Louise Fitzhugh

Twayne's United States Authors Series
Children's Literature

Ruth K. MacDonald, Editor
Purdue University Calumet

TUSAS 589

Louise Fitzhugh, 1964. *Reproduced by permission of the photographer, Susanne Singer.*

Louise Fitzhugh

Virginia L. Wolf
University of Wisconsin–Stout

Twayne Publishers • New York
Maxwell Macmillan Canada • Toronto
Maxwell Macmillan International • New York Oxford Singapore Sydney

Louise Fitzhugh
Virginia L. Wolf

Copyright 1991 by Twayne Publishers

Twayne Publishers
Macmillan Publishing Company
866 Third Avenue
New York, NY 10022

Maxwell Macmillan Canada, Inc.
1200 Eglinton Avenue East
Suite 200
Don Mills, Ontario M3C 3N1

Macmillan Publishing Company is part of the Maxwell Communication
Group of Companies.

Copyediting supervised by Barbara Sutton.
Book production by Janet Z. Reynolds.
Typeset by Compset, Inc., Beverly, Massachusetts.

10 9 8 7 6 5 4 3 2 1

The paper used in this publication meets the minimum requirements
of American National Standard for Information Sciences—Permanence
of Paper for Printed Library Materials, ANSI Z39.48-1984. ∞™

Printed and bound in the United States of America.

Library of Congress Cataloging-in-Publication Data

Wolf, Virginia L.
    Louise Fitzhugh / Virginia L. Wolf
        p.   cm. — (Twayne's United States authors series ; TUSAS
589. Children's literature)
    Includes bibliographical references (p.   ) and index.
    ISBN 0-8057-7614-1
    1. Fitzhugh, Louise—Criticism and interpretation.   2. Children's
stories, American—History and criticism.   I. Title.   II. Series:
Twayne's United States authors series ; TUSAS 589.   III. Series:
Twayne's United States authors series.   Children's literature.
PS3556.I8554Z76   91-22031

*For all the "different" children of the world,
may they all grow in love.*

Contents

Preface

Harriet the Spy is Louise Fitzhugh's claim to fame. Some people also know Fitzhugh's other children's books. Many children, for example, are avid fans of *Sport,* and recently one important critic praised *The Long Secret.*[1] Few people, however, know that Fitzhugh was a prolific painter and also wrote for adults. Indeed, almost no one knows much about her life nor about its impact on her writing and painting.

Before I begin discussing what I discovered and how I did so, I want to say a bit about myself as a writer. I do not claim to be objective. Since Heisenberg stated his Principle of Uncertainty,[2] scientists have increasingly acknowledged that human perception filters and colors our knowledge of the physical world. Faced with such a shift in epistemology, contemporary literary theorists take as their premise the inevitable subjectivity of interpretation. So do I. I am quite aware that my background, personality, and outlook determine my choice and treatment of subjects, especially in the case of this book. In acknowledging my subjectivity, however, I am not evading responsibility for a thorough and reasonable examination of my subject, nor am I abandoning the quest for truth. With the knowledge, understanding, emotions, skills, and training I possess, I have interpreted Louise Fitzhugh and her work to the best of my ability. I do not, however, believe that *my* truth about her and her art is *the* truth, even though it is the best that I can comprehend and communicate at this time in this place. Consequently, I announce my presence in this book and invite readers to agree, question, or disagree with me. Such openness about my personal involvement seems not only honest, but necessary, given current understanding of the nature of knowledge.

When I began this study, I was aware that attempts to discover additional information about Fitzhugh had not met with much success, but I was intrigued. Because it reminded me of my own childhood, *Harriet the Spy* had long been among my favorite children's books, and for just as long, I had suspected that Harriet was a portrait of Louise Fitzhugh as a child—in her personality and her obsession with writing. Also, on the basis of my own and several other lesbians' responses to this book, I had long suspected that Fitzhugh was gay. I had, in other words, identified myself with Fitzhugh, largely on the basis of her creation of Harriet. Certainly, my sense of kinship sparked my interest in writing this book. The one troubling item on my agenda was to track down the rumor in children's literature circles that Fitzhugh had committed suicide.

Naively expecting answers to questions about her sexual orientation and possible suicide, as well as to many less difficult questions, I sent out many letters. Responses were few and guarded. Several who answered referred me to Lois Morehead as her executor and to Marijane Meaker (M. E. Kerr) as her friend. Fitfully, the mystery began to unravel, as I heard from, in addition to Lois Morehead and Marijane Meaker, Ann Blecken, Alixe Gordin, Barbara Phelan, Frederica Fulton Leser, Charlotte Zolotow, Connie Francis, James Merrill, Peter Taylor, Joan Williams, Peggy Carroll, Charles McNutt, and various officials in the courthouse, the library, the Hutchinson School, and so forth in Memphis.

I extend thanks to all of these. In particular, I thank Marijane Meaker for being the first person willing to write an honest— indeed, blunt—response to my letter of inquiry. She pointed out that in asking about Fitzhugh's sexual orientation and possible suicide in the same letter, I implied a dark view of being a lesbian (which I certainly had not intended), and she made it very clear that Fitzhugh had not committed suicide. I am especially grateful to Lois Morehead for sharing the manuscripts "Mother Sweet, Father Sweet" and "Crazybaby" and a copy of the program for the Fitzhugh memorial service. For all of the time she spent talking to me, looking up information I requested, and providing me with the names of others to contact, I am most grateful to Alixe Gordin.

Without her help, this book could never have been written. I also owe a considerable debt to several critics for their wise and sensitive appraisals of Fitzhugh's writing, Perry Nodelman and Hamida Bosmajian in particular. Additionally important to my completion of this project were my editors Ruth MacDonald and Liz Fowler. I thank them for giving me extra time and for their patience and understanding. I thank the people in Research and Promotion at the University of Wisconsin–Stout for the same. Not only did they give me a grant, but then they extended my deadline twice and allowed me to revise what I had originally planned to do with the money. Finally, I wish to thank Carol Schumacher, George Shannon and David Holter, Michael Levy and Sandra Lindow, and Kathleen Horning for listening and reading and listening and reading. No one writes well without a caring, supportive, but critical community such as they always provide—even when I am quarrelsome.

Although difficult, writing this book has been one of the most rewarding activities of my life. The research has been a true adventure, including dead ends, fortuitous circumstances, unexpected breakthroughs, amazing discoveries, and—the end result of all adventure—increased self-knowledge. Although I had not anticipated enjoying biographical research, I found the process enormously stimulating, so much so that I fantasize about some day writing about it at length. For the purpose of this book, however, only what I discovered and what I have made of it are important.

My basic hypothesis that *Harriet the Spy* is largely autobiographical turned out to be true. Indeed, I was surprised to discover how thoroughly—if unpredictably—autobiographical Fitzhugh's writing is. Names, characters, places, and events often have a basis in her life. More important, the principal themes in her work suggest her resolution of conflicts that threatened her psychological well-being. As I had suspected, all of her work had much to do with her being an outsider.

I did not suspect, however, that an unhappy childhood was the primary reason she wrote. It makes sense, of course, that her nonconformity as an adult would have been to some extent evident in her personality as a child and might have resulted in her feeling rejected. She was not, however, a visible nonconformist as a youngster. In any case, the psychological damage she experienced went deeper than can be accounted for by nonconformity as a child and adolescent. I am convinced it began when she was very young and her father took her from her mother. Her demons were so severe that they suggest a breakdown in the attachment and separation process that occurs primarily during the first two years of life.

As an adult, she achieved some peace, mostly in the discovery of a community of artists (outsiders) and by means of writing and painting. She celebrated who she was as a child, satirized all those who rejected her, and exorcised her demons. In her children's books, she did so with warmth and humor, accepting or pitying even while poking fun at humanity. In other words, she was able to balance the pain she experienced as a child with understanding of human limitation. *Harriet the Spy*, in fact, did not prepare me for Fitzhugh's painful childhood. Nor did any of her other children's books. They are funny and upbeat and seldom sorrowful or bitter. Even *Nobody's Family Is Going to Change* is an angry, not a sad book. Still, anger is merely a self-protective response to pain, and all of Fitzhugh's despair over her childhood is there in her work—if one only scratches the surface.

I just didn't want to see it—perhaps because I had over identified with Fitzhugh. As the biographical evidence increased, my enthusiasm for writing this book evaporated, and I nearly abandoned it. I even began to question my understanding of *Harriet the Spy*. If Fitzhugh were severely damaged and, consequently, haunted by her childhood, so my thinking ran, how could she have written such a wise book. The logic of that thinking, I eventually realized, is not very good. As Anthony Storr clearly shows, trouble—indeed, despair—often motivates artistic creation because expressing pain and acquiring understanding can ease, indeed, heal, a wounded heart.[3] Despite my very human wish to deny Louise Fitzhugh's suffering as a child and her consequent psychological scars as an adult, eventually I came to my senses.

It is not that simple, of course, but the complexity lies in the following pages where I analyze the relationship between the details of her life and her work. There I express my hard won understanding of and enhanced appreciation for Fitzhugh's children's books.

Chronology

1928 Guston T. Fitzhugh, Jr., uncle of Louise Fitzhugh, publishes *Reveries,* a book of poetry 2 September. Louise Fitzhugh is born 5 October in Memphis, Tennessee, to Millsaps and Louise Perkins Fitzhugh.

1930 Her parents' divorce is granted 17 October, 15 months after the decree on 12 July 1929. Grandparents purchase Samarkand at 64 Rose Road in Red Acres, near Memphis, where Louise and her father live until he marries. They spend the summers in Miami, Florida.

1932 Begins school at Miss Hutchinson's.

1933 Millsaps Fitzhugh marries Sally Taylor on 14 October; Louise's mother begins appearing at Samarkand and elsewhere, trying to see Louise.

1937 Samarkand burns beyond repair; the Fitzhughs move to 2221 Poplar Avenue.

1940 Her grandfather, Captain Guston T. Fitzhugh, dies on 16 January.

1946 Graduates from Miss Hutchinson's; attends Southwestern College in Memphis.

1947 Attends Florida Southern College in Lakeland.

1948 Attends Bard College, majoring in literature and then child psychology.

1949 Her grandmother, Josie Millsaps Fitzhugh, dies 23 January.

1951 Leaves Bard College, six months short of graduation; moves to New York City to begin a career as a painter.

1952   Studies at the Art Students League and Cooper Union.

1953   Father becomes U.S. district attorney for West Tennessee.

1954   Travels in France.

1955   Meets Alixe Gordin; lives in apartment at 84 James Street in Greenwich Village.

1955–56 Exhibits her paintings at various branches of the New York Public Library and at the Sixty-second Street Gallery, Village Art Center, Panoras Gallery, and Downtown Community School. Completes an 18-by-18-foot mural in the hall of an apartment house on West Fourth Street.

1956–57 Studies flute and fresco painting in Bologna, Italy.

1957   Resides in apartment in the twenties on Lexington Avenue.

1959   Resides in apartment at 331 East Seventeenth Street where she writes *Suzuki Beane* with Sandra Scoppetone. Rents a storefront for use as a studio on Avenue B; paints people in the neighborhood, especially a Puerto Rican family and in particular their preschool son.

1961   *Suzuki Beane,* illustrated by Fitzhugh, is published by Doubleday. Fitzhugh's Seventeenth Street apartment is robbed; she moves to a railroad flat at 524 East Eighty-fifth Street where she writes *Harriet the Spy,* possibly *Sport,* and an unpublished novel she calls "Amelia."

1962   Fitzhugh's Uncle Gus dies in Memphis on 8 March.

1963   Has one-woman show at the Banfer Gallery in New York, 8–25 May; rents a summer cottage in Water Mill, meets Lois Morehead.

1964   *Harriet the Spy* published by Harper & Row. Fitzhugh moves to 80th Street and East End Avenue; spends summer in a cottage at Swan's Point, south of Water Mill.

1965   Spends summer in a rented house in Quoque, New York. Her father dies 7 October, leaving her four-fifths of his estate, which is valued at more than $1 million; *The Long Secret* is published by Harper & Row.

1967   Her stepmother dies 17 March and leaves most of her estate to Louise, including the family home in Memphis. Buys a summer home in Cutchogue on northern Long Island. Some time afterward, the manuscript of "Amelia" disappears from this house.

1969   Takes up residence in Bridgewater, Connecticut; spends the winters here and summers in the Hamptons. *Bang, Bang, You're Dead,* by Fitzhugh and Scoppetone, illustrated by Fitzhugh, is published by Harper & Row.

1974   Dies 19 November in Bridgewater; *Nobody's Family Is Going to Change* is published by Farrar, Straus & Giroux.

1978   *I Am Five* is published by Delacorte; *The Tap Dance Kid,* based on *Nobody's Family Is Going to Change,* is produced as an after-school special by Learning Corporation.

1979   *Sport* is published by Delacorte.

1982   *I Am Three,* illustrated by Susanna Natti, and *I Am Four,* illustrated by Susan Bonner, are published by Delacorte.

1983   *The Tap Dance Kid* (unrelated to its earlier namesake), script by Charles Blackwell, also based on *Nobody's Family Is Going to Change,* opens on Broadway at the Broadhurst Theater on 21 December.

1984   *The Tap Dance Kid* moves to the Minskoff Theatre on 27 March and wins Tony Awards for best book for a musical, for outstanding choreography, for outstanding featured actor in a musical, and for best actor in a secondary role.

1988 The play *Harriet the Spy*, adapted by Leslie Brody, is produced by the Children's Theatre Company in Minneapolis; runs 5 February to 2 April.

Acknowledgments

I would like to thank Harper & Row for granting permission to reprint for the market of the United States, its territories, the Philippine Islands, Canada, and the open market, excluding the British Commonwealth, specified text excerpts and illustrations from pp. 23 and 55 from *Harriet the Spy,* © 1964 by Louise Fitzhugh; specified text excerpts and illustrations from pp. 90 and 248 from *The Long Secret,* © 1965 by Louise Fitzhugh; cover illustration and illustration from page 28 from *Bang, Bang, You're Dead* by Louise Fitzhugh and Sandra Scoppetone, pictures © 1969 by Louise Fitzhugh.

I would also like to thank Victor Gollancz, Ltd., for permission to reprint the specified text excerpts and illustrations from *Harriet the Spy* and *The Long Secret* for the market of the British Commonwealth.

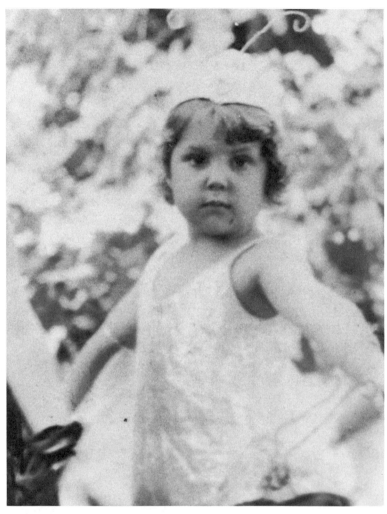

Enlarged and reproduced from a photograph of Louise Fitzhugh's first grade class at Miss Hutchinson's, provided by Mrs. W. P. Morrison, alumni representative of the class of 1946.

1

Portrait of the Artist as an Outsider

The Mystery

Those of us who know Louise Fitzhugh's work for children and who wish to know who she was will find nothing in print that allows us insight into the sources of her writing and illustrations. The standard reference works such as *Something about the Author, Contemporary Authors,* and *Twentieth-Century Writers for Children,* of course, only briefly recite the facts of her external life. In addition, there is Perry Nodelman's lengthy article about her life and work for the *Dictionary of Literary Biography.* It adds somewhat to our knowledge of Fitzhugh—telling us that she had an unhappy childhood, even though her family was wealthy; that she hated the South, where she was born and grew up; that she left her childhood home as soon as she could; and that she had many talents besides writing and drawing, including painting, dancing, playing the flute, and tennis. Still, Fitzhugh essentially remains a mystery.

My correspondence and telephone conversations with those who knew her did relieve this mystery. However, many I wrote did not even respond, and those who did were sometimes very guarded or asked that their names not be used. Based on all the information at hand, and from what her friends have said of her, it is apparent that Fitzhugh was a lesbian. I suspect many I contacted were trying to conceal her sexual orientation. Others spoke openly of her as a lesbian and provided information that greatly expands what is currently known about Fitzhugh. There are, nevertheless, very apparent gaps and contradictions in the information I gathered. Few who knew her as a child responded or wished to be identified—only Peter Taylor, her stepuncle and a famous writer himself; Ann Blecken, who knew her from kindergarten through high school; Peggy Carroll and Charles McNutt, who knew her during high school; and Joan Williams, a fellow student at Bard College and also a Southerner and writer. Her friends in New York City were the primary sources of information. Fitzhugh emerges as a fascinating woman and artist from the descriptions and stories of those who wrote or called me, but, certainly, some of this fascination arises from what some did not say and from what I can only surmise.

The picture of Fitzhugh that follows is a reconstruction. Any attempt at biography is, of course, always an interpretation, that is, the biographer's view of the person. Calling attention to the suppositional element inherent in biography is here perhaps more necessary than in some cases, however, because my account of Fitzhugh's life is a composite of what many have told me and because I never knew Louise Fitzhugh personally or had the opportunity to read at length the materials she left at her death. Whenever I have filled in gaps or resolved contradictions in what Fitzhugh's friends said of her, I have relied heavily on what she wrote as a guide to surmising what she might have done, said, or felt. Other useful guidance comes from my understanding of artistic development and motivation in four general groups: females, homosexuals, satirists, and writers for children.[1]

A Gay, Female, Satirical Artist

For many reasons, Louise Fitzhugh was an outsider. As many scholars note,[2] feeling outside the dominant culture has characterized serious artists of the twentieth century. Fitzhugh was ad-

ditionally female and gay. It is not surprising that she turned to
satire in both her writing and her drawing and painting, for satire
is the form of writing that best expresses an artist's sense of
alienation from society.[3] If Feinberg is correct in his understanding of the personalities of famous satirists,[4] Fitzhugh was a satirist as a result of temperament and not of choice. He contends
that the gift for satire is innate and that from a young age famous
satirists are intensely aware of and delighted by being different
from other people, resulting in a fascination with incongruities
and contradictions. There is evidence about Fitzhugh's childhood
that supports our seeing her as like other satirists. There is also
evidence in her books for children.

Critics have long realized that many books for children are *Bil-
dungsromane*, and it is only reasonable to assume that books intended for this audience would take growing up as one of their
primary subjects. The *Bildungsroman*, as Jerome Hamilton
Buckley points out in *Seasons of Youth: The Bildungsroman from
Dickens to Golding*, is "highly autobiographical"[5] and, therefore,
"has also frequently been a kind of *Künstlerroman*," (Buckley,
111) telling of an artist's growing up. In children's literature, the
situation is surely often the same and is obviously so in Fitzhugh's work, where there are one or more characters who perform
as artists in every book but *Bang, Bang, You're Dead*, in which
the children's play is very like theater and art.[6] *Suzuki Beane*
portrays a family of artists and another family of patrons.[7] In
Fitzhugh's first two novels (*Harriet the Spy* and *The Long Secret*),[8] her protagonists are the developing writer, Harriet, and the
developing artist, Beth Ellen. Willie and his uncle in *Nobody's
Family Is Going to Change* are dancers,[9] Sport's dad is a writer,[10]
and the children in *I Am Three, I Am Four,* and *I Am Five* all
engage in drawing and storytelling.[11] In her many portraits of
artists, Fitzhugh was clearly preoccupied with why a person became an artist and with what it meant to be one.

None of her artist characters really choose their professions so
much as they are driven to them. They are all outsiders—misfits
in one way or another because of their family situations and their
preoccupation with their art. They are also all, to varying degrees,
angry. Anger is, in fact, a subterranean theme in all of Fitzhugh's

books, and in *Nobody's Family Is Going to Change* (published only a few days after her death), anger erupts to the surface. In all of her work, Fitzhugh blasts away at society for not valuing art and artists sufficiently, just as she shows that what we value—riches, comfort, and conformity, in particular—is often meaningless. All of her art is satirical, arising from her view as an outsider and from her anger.

But to describe her work as that of an angry outsider is to miss what it also is—a celebration of the joys and satisfactions of being who one really is. The very fiber of Fitzhugh's best writing and illustration is a healthy egocentricity.

Her Family

Her temperament at birth may account for her becoming a satirist, but so may her early environment. If she did have an unhappy childhood, one that her books for children often reflect in one way or another, it was also a privileged childhood. She never suffered any lack of material possessions. Also, although they criticized her for nonconformity, her very eccentric family implicitly provided her with permission to be whatever she wished. Privilege, in other words, supported Fitzhugh's becoming rather thoroughly egocentric.

On her father's side, her family is an old, respected, wealthy one of Memphis. Her father and grandfather were lawyers, active in politics and civic affairs. Guston T. Fitzhugh, her grandfather, acquired wealth in his marriage to Josie Millsaps, granddaughter of the famous Reuben Millsaps, a war hero and founder of Millsaps College in Jackson, Mississippi, where both grandparents were born and reared. Following in his father's footsteps, Millsaps Fitzhugh, Louise's father, eventually became U.S. district attorney in Memphis. But while on a tour after graduation from Emory University, he violated his family's expectations. He met and married Louise Perkins, a young woman who wished to be a tap dancer and whom his parents considered socially below him. The marriage lasted about a year and produced on 5 October 1928 one child, Louise Fitzhugh. The divorce was followed by a custody fight with all the cards stacked in favor of Louise's father. Louise told her friends that he kidnapped her from her mother and used all the resources of his own father's legal, political, and social power to obtain custody. It may also be true that her mother tried to kidnap her back. This period was surely traumatic for the child. Her mother disappeared (Peter Taylor said that she had a nervous breakdown and later went to Hollywood to try her luck as a dancer) and then returned and began trying to see her.

The first years of Fitzhugh's life, during which she lived in her grandparents' old mansion, became the vital substance of her children's books. For several years, she told friends, she believed her mother dead. Then her mother defied the Fitzhughs and asked to see Louise. In response to the Fitzhughs' refusal, she began showing up at places where Louise might be alone or with understanding people who would let her see her daughter. Peter Taylor remembers his discomfort when Louise's mother once appeared unexpectedly at the home of Mary Holmes, Louise's aunt. According to Ann Blecken, Louise saw her mother on a regular basis during all the years that Ann and Louise were friends, so some arrangement with the Fitzhughs must have eventually been achieved. But most of those whom I contacted remembered experiences with Louise or stories she told of her childhood that suggest that many of the bizarre events in Fitzhugh's books were actual events in her childhood.

As a result of these events, she was often frightened and insecure. The somewhat disguised autobiography of her fiction reveals that a chief feeling during these years was loneliness. Both her friends' stories and Fitzhugh's fiction also suggest an amazing courage and vitality, which Peter Taylor confirmed in his contribution to her memorial service at St. James Church in New York City. In his words, "circumstances and her temperament made Louise discover early that if she were ever to know real independence and enjoy the satisfaction of developing her special talents, she would have to wage war—sometimes defensive and sometimes aggressive—against the smothering influence of a large Southern family."

Adult Fiction as Autobiography

At her death, Fitzhugh left two works she intended for adults, an unfinished novel called "Crazybaby" and a completed play called "Mother Sweet, Father Sweet." The novel is incomplete. It is broken into two parts, with the last half using the same names for characters as does the play. There are several versions of some parts of the novel. The play, copyrighted in 1962, is a finished work, obviously about the same family but set before the events of the novel. Both of these, she told her friends, were based on her own childhood. Few remain who can corroborate her version of her childhood, and none of these did so entirely. Ultimately, of course, it is her version that counts anyway—her memories creating for her the reality she both loved and hated, the reality she needed to understand. Certainly, because she told the same story over and over with what seems like neurotic repetition, her reader becomes convinced that—no matter how it really was—this is the way it was for the child Louise in the memory of the adult Louise.

The play and novel are about a young child who lives in a large Southern mansion with her grandmother, uncle, and a few trusted black servants. A father is somewhere in the background, and in the play, so is a mother, a woman whom the child does not know and does not wish to be with. The child also rejects her father, who in the play is selfish and immature. He is interested in his daughter only because she is special to her grandparents. Similarly, they want her not for herself, but rather because the grandmother seeks a replacement for a daughter who died as a child and the grandfather will do anything his wife demands. If the mother seems weak and the father and grandfather cruel, the grandmother and the uncle are insane—more definitely and bizarrely so in the novel than in the play. The grandmother in the novel considers herself queen of the birds and daily throws them dollar bills from her upstairs window. The uncle is obese, speaks in rhyme, and is suicidal. Once he buys every razor blade in stock at the drugstore the family owns. Aunt Dolly patrols the house, looking for signs of instability so that she can—with the child's father's help—put both the grandmother and the uncle in an institution and thereby possess the family money. There is no aunt in the play. There is, however, an uncle who is emotionally unstable and a poet, tormented by his father's and his brother's rejection and desirous of providing his niece contact with her mother.

Fitzhugh had a real Uncle Gus, upon whom these fictional uncles were based. Her Aunt Mary, with whom she stayed as a young child, playing with her cousins Josie and Mary, seems an unlikely source of Aunt Dolly. Peter Taylor remembers the Holmes house as a place of refuge for little Louise and Louise's aunt as especially fond of her. On the other hand, Mr. Taylor did characterize Aunt Mary as a dramatic person, much as Aunt Dolly is in the play.

The settings in both manuscripts are similar—large, richly furnished, gothic mansions. Fitzhugh referred to her grandparents' home in her later years as the pink palace. There is, of course, the famous Pink Palace of Memphis, the estate built by Clarence Saunders, the founder of the Piggly-Wiggly chain. Samarkand, the Fitzhugh home on Rose Road in Red Acres, was large and ornate, but nowhere near as extravagant as the 155-acre Old Spanish Pink Palace off Central Avenue at Goodwyn. The exaggeration of Samarkand suggested by Fitzhugh's conscious or unconscious association of it with the Pink Palace surely reflects her experience of it as a child. The mansion in the novel and the play overwhelms the child. The staircase lined with old paintings of angry-looking ancestors and satyrs and the dark corners of the large rooms produce fear, as they will in grandparents' homes for both Beth Ellen in Fitzhugh's *The Long Secret* and Sport in her novel of the same name.

Finally, in both manuscripts, there is a lost, little girl. Fitzhugh calls her Crazybaby in the first half of the novel and Josie in the last half and in the play. Fitzhugh's grandmother's first name was Josie, and one of her Aunt Mary's daughters was her grandmother's namesake. The names here are richly suggestive of some of Fitzhugh's feelings about herself as a young child, for example, her confusion and uncertainty and her strong identification with her grandmother. But the behavior of the little girl is more important than her name. Frightened of the house she lives in and of the family she lives with, she looks for and receives abundant affection from a busy black servant—Teacake in the novel and Clint in the play. As a child, she was very fond of her black nanny and of the Fitzhugh's black chauffeur.

"Mother Sweet, Father Sweet"

The child is a pawn and background character in "Mother Sweet, Father Sweet," whose protagonist is her Uncle Jake Phelan.[12] He is a young, thin, physically healthy poet, whose mother has committed him on several occasions to a mental hospital. As his father, Judge Phelan (Fitzhugh's grandfather was always called Captain), points out to Josie's father, Maxwell, the key to Mrs. Phelan's decisions to do so is Jake's having embarrassed her socially. The plot of the play, then, involves the two men's looking for a chance to create a situation that will convince Mrs. Phelan to commit Jake again, while Jake looks for a way to discredit his brother. If he can regain his father's respect (and money), Jake plans to leave Memphis forever with his lover, Sweet. In New York, she will pursue a career as a singer and he one as a poet. This future depends on his showing his father that Maxwell is a bad father and person, who does not deserve custody of Josie, a plan motivated in part because Jake vaguely identifies with Josie and recognizes that no one in his family loves her. He hopes that her mother might. By the end of the play, after her mother, her maternal grandmother, and Uncle Jake try to kidnap Josie and after they discredit Maxwell in his father's eyes and drive him off, it is obvious indeed that only Clint really cares for Josie. The maternal grandmother is an obese, low-class, racing fanatic, similar to Mama Jenkins in *Nobody's Family Is Going to Change* and clearly based on Fitzhugh's real maternal grandmother, whom she visited a few times with her mother. Even Jake—if only misguidedly—uses the child as a pawn in his efforts to regain his parents' love and respect.

Several undercurrents are, of course, implicit in these events. Neither of the sons is loved; both instead constantly jockey for position with their father. The mother is the center of the family, her power and possessiveness becoming increasingly obvious as the play progresses. His desire not to upset his wife controls Judge Phelan's behavior with his sons. Although the Judge and Maxwell Phelan wish to get rid of Jake, they do so in a back-handed way because he is his mother's favorite son—with suggestions, in tone, if not in act, of incest. At the end of the play, she finally has him as she wants him. Returned from the institution, he has this time given up. Obese and whining, he sits and dozes as his mother reads him *Peter Rabbit.*

Josie, who has been the object of all her grandmother's attention throughout the play, is ignored after Jake's return. Mrs. Phelan's desire to possess a child was the key to Josie's status. At various points in the play, we see her in charge of Josie, teaching her French and piano and everything she needs to be just like her grandmother. Once when the grandmother is drunk, there are here, too, sexual overtones in her behavior. We also see her cruelty when the child does not perform as expected. At one point she closes the piano on Josie's hand because she cannot play as well as her grandmother did as a child. (Mrs. Josie Millsaps Fitzhugh was an accomplished musician, as was Louise Fitzhugh.) On the whole, Josie, who is five in the play, seems remarkably tough—if also frightened and hurt at times. She rejects her grandfather's and father's every phoney attempt to show affection for her, often kicking them in the shin. She also rejects her mother and maternal grandmother, and by the end of the play she refuses to call her paternal grandmother "mother," as she had before. Now she says Sweet is really her mother and vows to get away from the Phelans as soon as she is old enough. In effect, she rejects her family, asserts her identity as an outsider, and seems pleased with herself as such.

"Crazybaby"

The pain and confusion and anger one would expect of a child in this situation is more obvious in the novel than in the play, especially at its beginning. In the first part of the novel, the child's only name is Crazybaby, and she is not a member of the family but a runaway, whose drunken father beat and otherwise abused her. She came to the Birdsong mansion begging for food, and Teacake took her in and got Mrs. Birdsong to agree to her staying. Teacake is the center of this child's world. Crazybaby obeys and loves her without question, for apparently no one else has ever cared for or about her. She has clearly been more affected by her environment than has Josie in the play. Like her adoptive grandmother and uncle, she, too, is at least somewhat "crazy." Besides what her name suggests, she has moments of acute terror, often associated with fear of dying. Also she never finishes most of her drawings, which decorate every scrap of paper and every hidden portion of the house, because she believes that her completed drawing of a person will result in his death. When at one point her hatred of a fat, red faced, hypocritical white man leads her to draw him entirely, he does, in fact, have a stroke.

Later in the novel, when her name has become Josie Birdsong and she is identified as being eight years old, the focus shifts from her to the family and to a plot somewhat like that of the play, suggesting that Fitzhugh's role in the family drama was more that of an observer than a participant. Some of the differences in plot between the two works result because the events of the novel occur after those of the play. Mr. Birdsong is dead, and Byron, Josie's uncle, is like Jake at the end of the play—obese and resigned. Mrs. Birdsong delights in her son's creativity (he speaks in rhyme) and in her birds. She seems harmlessly insane, requiring six of everything to dine and to dress. She is also a diabetic, requiring daily insulin shots. Teacake is in charge of this house. Jason, Josie's father, lives in New York, and Dolly, another character so bizarre she is funny, plots to get both Mrs. Birdsong and Byron committed so that she and Jason can get the family money. (Mrs. Fitzhugh did, in fact, leave her money to her nurse, and Louise's father and aunt did, in fact, successfully contest the will.) What really marks the play and novel as different is tone. The novel is a farce (especially the last half), a burlesque of the play's devastingly ironic tragedy.

The judgment of family in "Mother Sweet, Father Sweet" is unflinching. There is no sympathy for the parents and little for Maxwell, his wife, or her mother. Jake gets some admiration and compassion, but ultimately, he is the victim. His childhood has left him unequipped for survival as an independent artist. The only hope left at the end of the play is that Josie may escape. Louise Fitzhugh did, of course, and one must suspect that her uncle (in fantasy, if not in actuality) provided her with a model of both how not and how to do so. Clearly, the way out, as she saw it, was to reject the family, as he did not, and to be different and creative—to be an artist and an outsider, as he was.

Just as clearly, the way to fail was to care about and to believe in the family. The difficulty in avoiding this failure is already implicit in "Crazybaby." Her name, her terror, and her guilt about drawing suggest that she has, to some extent, accepted the family's judgment of her. Also she, like Teacake, sides with the family against her father and Dolly—largely perhaps because Teacake's and her survival depends on keeping Mrs. Birdsong and Byron together as a family. In any case, the grandmother is treated more kindly and the uncle less tragically than they are in the play, although when at the end Byron takes up with a woman and Mrs. Birdsong rejects him, we see the same unhealthy possessiveness that characterized the grandmother in the play.

The novel breaks off at this point—perhaps because Fitzhugh did not know where to go with the revelation of Mrs. Birdsong's character as more sinister than the novel had before suggested. Similarly, she did not seem to know what to do with the implications in the early part of the novel that Crazybaby is insane, for these get forgotten about halfway through the novel. Jason, the father, also seems less a villain than Maxwell—more a bungling conformist and less selfish and weak-kneed. Here his mother's overt rejection earns him some sympathy. Dolly is the only villain in the novel, and her simplistic motivation—greed—makes her less frightening than Judge and Mrs. Phelan. As people who use their children's love and need as a source of power, they are believably and terrifyingly evil.

Her Children's Books as Autobiography

"Crazybaby" seems more like *Sport* than like any of Fitzhugh's other books. It is comic melodrama, glorying in the bizarre and eccentric. In "Mother Sweet, Father Sweet," the other side of Fitzhugh wins out. The angry satirist takes control and shows with profundity and without mercy the selfishness and the destructiveness of this family. Taken together, the novel and play more accurately express who Fitzhugh was and better reflect the attitudes she repeatedly expressed in her children's novels than either does separately. The work closest to "Mother Sweet, Father Sweet" is *Nobody's Family Is Going to Change*. The other books seem both less farcical than *Sport* and "Crazybaby" and less angry than *Nobody's Family Is Going to Change* and "Mother Sweet, Father Sweet."

Even more important, in these two similarly and relatively straightforward autobiographical pieces, we find abundant proof that Fitzhugh's children's books were also heavily autobiographical. Many, many details in her work came from her life—the fat maternal grandmother, the nurturing black servants, tap dancing, and so forth. All of Fitzhugh's writing is of a piece. Harriet M. Welsch, her most memorable character, is a loner and an artist, who feels most loved by and most loves a servant. Harriet's egocentricity, lack of compassion, and unfettered honesty are the very qualities that make Josie and, to a lesser extent, Crazybaby survivors. In Beth Ellen Hanson, we see another version of Crazybaby—secretly angry and guilty, afraid to declare herself an artist. Fittingly enough, Beth Ellen's grandmother is more like Crazybaby's grandmother than like Josie's—distant and confusing, but not cruel.

Like the Phelans or Birdsongs, most of the families are wealthy in Fitzhugh's children's novels. Two of the children are very rich as a result of grandparents. These two, Beth Ellen and Sport, find their grandparents' houses large and intimidating. They also have parents who show interest in them only because wealthy grandparents make parenthood a requirement of inheritance. Interesting enough, these parents are both women. The only good mother, in fact, in all of Fitzhugh's books, unless one counts Ole Golly and Beth Ellen's grandmother, is Kate, Sport's stepmother. Fitzhugh went after a father only in *Nobody's Family Is Going to Change,* although Harriet's too busy, executive father and Beth

Ellen's absent father are distant versions of William Sheridan, the father in *Nobody's Family Is Going to Change*. One can also see a distant resemblance between her uncle and both Sport's writer father and Uncle Dipsey Bates, the dancer in *Nobody's Family Is Going to Change*. Both of these men are sensitive innocents, who cannot handle the child protagonist's family and whose greatest joy is their art. In other words, many of Fitzhugh's repertoire of characters, who all verge toward types, had their roots in her childhood.

Common Themes
There are several other parallels between these two manuscripts and the children's novels. Most important of all, like the adult manuscripts Fitzhugh's children's books all criticize families for requiring that children conform and for denying their individual identities. Her satire is consistently of parents and a society that stifle and repress children, inhibiting, if not eradicating, individuality and creativity. Quite naturally, her most persuasive heroes are artists, usually female artists, whose values are in direct conflict with those of their families and of society. The energy and anger with which she attacks adult society for their resistance to and rejection of children's natural development link her to other gay artists, whose experience of repression and intolerance, especially as atypical children, makes them sharp-eyed observers and sharp-voiced critics of society. As Paul Binding says in *Lorca: The Gay Imagination,* "the sensibility that makes it so powerful a cry against all injustices must have been nurtured by . . . membership of a class which knew what rejection and denial meant, the homosexual."[13]

Similarly, in her work for both adults and children Fitzhugh's celebration of the artist, especially of the girl as incipient artist, not only counterbalances her satire and her anger, but also further places her within a gay tradition. Many critics point out that the artist is often the hero of gay art, to some extent because the artist, like the homosexual, seeks freedom from the expectations of traditional gender roles (Binding, 97–100).[14] As Maurice Beebe suggests, the male artist has always portrayed himself as sensitive, dreamy, passive, bookish, egocentric, tormented, and mis-understood.[15] And as Huf adds, "artist heroines by women are athletic in build, skilled in sports, unshrinking in fights, able in mathematics, plucky in love, and daring in sexual adventures" (Huf, 4). Finally, as Binding points out about Lorca and his circle of artist friends, many of whom were gay, their "art is frequently concerned, and at profound levels, with transpositions of accepted sexual roles and androgyny" (Binding, 97). The homosexual, of course, often suffers much more for failure to comply with the appropriate gender role than the heterosexual man or woman. The lesbian is often judged inadequately feminine and the gay man, inadequately masculine. Therefore, both become aware of the repression and distortion of traditional gender roles and may come to see the advantages of freedom from the demands of these roles and, consequently, other conventional behavior imposed by society that does not come naturally to the individual. In other words, nonconformity, especially gender nonconformity, as impor-tant as it is for the heterosexual artist, is often much more im-portant for the homosexual artist.

Certainly Fitzhugh rather thoroughly rejects conventional be-havior. At its core, her work celebrates the free spirit, savoring any signs of authenticity. Among her characters, children are more often authentic than are the adults, the adult artist being an obvious exception. But the character she most relishes is clearly the girl as artist, a character whom Huf identifies as al-most nonexistent in literature before the twentieth century (Huf, 1–2). The egocentricity of the artist, his self-absorption, Beebe points out, sets him apart from us, but because it allows him to create for us illuminating and moving visions of ourselves, we do not reject him for it, but rather praise him as the exceptional hu-man being—a creator (Beebe, 13–16). Huf explores the contradic-tions of such egocentricity for females, seeing the dilemma posed by these contradictions as responsible for the relatively small number of female artists in the past (Huf, 5–14). The female role, as traditionally understood in Western culture, requires self-sacrifice and caring for others. Such an ethic obviously conflicts squarely with the egocentricity we expect of and even celebrate in modern artists. But in the twentieth century, traditional gender roles have been under attack, and many more women have become artists and asserted the importance of their own egos. Important to the portrait of the female as artist, Huf points out (and Fitzhugh's work exemplifies), is her accepting, exploring, and glorying in her own egocentricity (Huf, 11).

The Passage to Adulthood

Certainly, there are many signs of conflict in Fitzhugh's life after her early childhood. Eventually, her father remarried, and Louise lived with him and Sally Taylor, his wife, until Louise left Memphis. This marriage brought her father into conformity with his parents' and upper-crust Southern society's expectations, but it also tightened the restrictions on Louise. She told her New York friends stories of her years at the Hutchinson School for young ladies (known then as Miss Hutchinson's), of being required to model clothes at the country club, and of being part of the court during the annual Cotton Carnival in Memphis. Her Memphis friends, Peggy Carroll and Ann Blecken, confirmed her popularity, if not all the details of the stories she told. They also noted that there was little sign that she was unhappy when they knew her. Fitzhugh claimed that because she did not want to follow her parents' wishes and become a debutante she ran off and married Ed Thompson. Louise asked Peggy Carroll, who knew Louise during high school, to go with her. Mrs. Carroll indicated that she was surprised when Louise told her she loved Ed. Everyone was apparently surprised, but no one had heard the version of this story Louise told later in New York. Her parents annulled the marriage, but, of course, by then she could not be a debutante. Mrs. Carroll suggested that the marriage may also have had something to do with a scandal about Louise and another female student, which the family responded to by getting the girl sent away and having the whole incident hushed up.

Similar signs of conflict may be evident in her movement from Southwestern College in Memphis to Florida Southern College,

Reproduced from a photograph of Louise Fitzhugh at age 16, provided by Mrs. W. P. Morrison, alumni representative of the class of 1946 at Miss Hutchinson's.

to Bard, to New York City. She experienced her father as very controlling, but gradually managed to put distance between herself and the South and to assert her identity as an individual, a lesbian, and an artist. In New York, she tried to support herself with a variety of jobs—mostly in sales. But she essentially lived on the $500-a-month trust fund established for her by her grandmother. This allowed her to train and work as a painter as she found her way into the community of Greenwich Village.

During her New York years, she was active socially with a group of artists and intellectuals, including Marijane Meaker (who writes for young people as M. E. Kerr), Sandra Scoppetone (also a writer for children), Maurice Sendak (noted author/illustrator of picture books such as *Where the Wild Things Are*), James Merrill (a Pulitzer Prize–winning poet), Lorraine Hansberry (noted author of works such as *Raisin in the Sun*), Alixe Gordin (a casting director for feature films), Frances Batterham (daughter of Kenneth Burke, the Marxist critic and philosopher), Fredericka Fulton Leser (an academic and an artist), Francis Hines (artist), Jane Wagner (noted playwright of such works as *The Search for Signs of Intelligent Life in the Universe*), and Connie Ford (an actress known for her role as Ada on the television soap opera "Another World"). In a letter to me, Meaker describes Fitzhugh as "one of the happiest people I've ever known . . . a real holiday, you know, a woman with great elan and passion. . . . Everyone adored Louise. She was generous and amusing and so quick to laugh at her own foibles, telling stories on herself and her relatives."

These years were good ones for Fitzhugh. She was at last able to be herself, to pursue a life-style she desired, and to work at being an artist. Her friends, unlike her family, were able to love and appreciate her as she was. Many with whom I spoke were overjoyed at the chance to relive their memories of her. Everyone remembers her as a great wit and conversationalist. Alixe Gordin, with whom she began a lifelong friendship in the mid-fifties, believes that Louise was never happier than when she was surrounded by this circle of intelligent, creative friends, engaged in thought-provoking or amusing discussion. These were also the years when she devoted herself to painting.

There is evidence, however, that her childhood, as anyone with knowledge of psychology would expect, continued to haunt her. Lois Morehead, her literary executor, describes Fitzhugh as painfully shy and her diaries as tortured. She says that the one word that best identifies Fitzhugh is *intense,* with *funny* running a close second. Morehead and other friends also point out that during all of the years after she came to New York, Fitzhugh was in analysis, dedicating *The Long Secret* to her analyst. Meaker believes that she was "not a tortured analysand" but "was always trying to understand her childhood." Meaker, like everyone who knew her well, describes her as a very sensitive person. Charlotte Zolotow, an editor who worked with her on *Harriet* and *The Long Secret,* remembers her as "moody and wonderful"; Fredericka Fulton Leser, as "a genuinely non-doctrinaire radical, a supremely difficult, emotionally complex person."

These contradictory descriptions of Fitzhugh certainly suggest that she was "emotionally complex," her happiness and achievements during the last half of her life always existing in tension with her continued efforts to come to terms with her childhood. These efforts, of course, were often works of art—painting or writing that expressed her demons. As Maurice Beebe points out in *Ivory Towers and Sacred Founts: The Artist as Hero in Fiction from Goethe to Joyce,* artists characterize themselves as divided between life and art, driven to create in order that they might live (having exorcised their demons), but kept from living by the need to create (Beebe, 21–64). The person and the artist in this conflict between life and art often seem quite different people, although not in the simplistic sense that only one side shows in life and the other in art. Such an analysis seems true of Fitzhugh. She was happy, generous, sensitive, and amusing; on the other hand, she was often angry, demanding, driven, depressed, and critical. But at her best, in her life and her art, she was able to resolve her ambivalence and balance both sides of her personality.

Her Painting

During her early years as a painter, especially after her year (1956–57) in Italy, where she traveled with Frances Batterham and studied mural techniques at the Academia di Bella Arte in Bologna, her paintings were very tormented. She decided on this trip after a quarrel with a lover. While there she became great friends with Fabio Rieti, a painter, and on her return indicated to Joan Williams that living as a lesbian was troubling her. Barbara Phelan, a New York friend, says that Louise offered to hang some of her paintings in Phelan's apartment but that she had to return them because she found she could not live with paintings expressing such pain. Fitzhugh, however, went through phases in her painting, moving in the late fifties and early sixties from these large, angry, Italianate paintings in intense color to drawings that, although still satiric, were lighter, with some pastels. Very fond of the German expressionists, she was always essentially preoccupied with the human form and distortions of it. She did almost no landscapes, although Alixe Gordin recalls one view of the dunes out of a window in Fitzhugh's home in Cutchogue, and Ursula Nordstrom in a letter to Perry Nodelman (Nodelman, 142) wrote of one of a little girl in a field of flowers. The use of ink during this second phase was very important, as was the focus on satire, especially of the rich and the fat. Both served as preparation for her eventual interest in book illustration. In yet a third phase, in the late sixties, she did several very fine portraits that showed much more careful attention to line and definition than had been true of her early work. At the same time, she did a series of very large, abstract paintings, some as large as four by five or six feet, that were very bright and light and warm, which she identified as expressive of emotions provoked by certain experiences; for example, she did one of making love.

Much of what she was capable of as a painter was revealed in her show at the Banfer Gallery in 1963, which a reviewer said demonstrated "a painter's feel, a satirist's eye, and a comic's hand. She depends substantially on line and a montage technique, assembling images, one memory overlying, giving way to another. *Two Salesladies Discussing God* in colored inks and synthetic resins resembles Mother ripened to vintage state in the cellar."[16] Her last paintings, a series that she called "the dolls," reflect her growth as an abstractionist and her continued interest in satire, here of socialization as a dehumanizing influence on women. Everyone speaks without hesitation about what an excellent painter she was. After her death, Julien Levy, the famous gallery owner largely responsible for the acceptance of surrealism in the United States, wrote for her memorial service that "her painting held all the promise in the world."

Her Writing

Fitzhugh did more painting than writing, but here, too, she was a divided person. Fredericka Fulton Leser said at Fitzhugh's memorial service, "It was as though the inner pressure to express herself was so intense that a single means or medium could not satisfy it." Her children's books, which she began writing in the late fifties (the first one was written with Sandra Scoppetone), reveal much the same tension as her painting—sometimes intense and angry, sometimes light and amusing, and sometimes a balance between the two. And like her painting, her published writing began and ended on the angry side with *Suzuki Beane* (1961) and *Nobody's Family Is Going to Change* (1974). The latter novel, like her doll paintings, reveals her great increase in skill, technique, and control, which makes its anger seem even more devastating than that of her early work. On the light side, there are all of the books published since her death: *I Am Five, Sport, I Am Three,* and *I Am Four.* One of these, *Sport,* was probably written in the late sixties. I was unable to discover when the others were written or the extent to which they were finished manuscripts, although I assume that Fitzhugh did little with them after she began *Nobody's Family Is Going to Change.* In any case, Fitzhugh achieved her greatest sense of balance in *Harriet the Spy* and *The Long Secret* in the mid-sixties, which was also true of her painting.

One can only speculate about why the early sixties were such productive and successful years for Fitzhugh. To some extent, the decision to be an artist, a large circle of artist friends, a significant relationship, a fair amount of respect for both her painting and writing, and the consequent feeling of freedom and well-being may sufficiently explain this period. Surely, also important was her need to prove herself to and to be financially independent of her father. His death in 1965 would then perhaps have relieved her of these pressures and of the need to be as intent on getting recognition for her work. With the interest from the trust he left her and with her royalties, she would be financially comfortable for the rest of her life. In any case, she was never again to show her paintings and only to publish two more children's books before she died in 1974, although she wrote or painted several hours nearly every day of her life.

In the early sixties, she moved out of the Village and into an apartment on East 85th Street, where *Harriet* was written and set. Here she may also have written *Sport,* which she offered to

Harper & Row in the late sixties or early seventies, but refused to revise as they recommended. In the early sixties, she also began to summer in the Hamptons, where she set *The Long Secret*. After her father's death, she bought a house in Cutchogue, where she then spent her summers. In the late sixties, she also gave up New York City in the winters, moving to Bridgewater, Connecticut. She enjoyed the peace, quiet, and security of this small village, spending much time walking.

Her Sexual Orientation

Fitzhugh was always fairly open about her sexual orientation. In the last years of her life, she dressed in clothes she had especially designed and tailored for herself—masculine attire essentially, trousers, vests, and boots. Her friends say that delighting in the strange and eccentric, she presented herself to the world as she was—a free spirit. When younger, her smallness, dress, and hair would have allowed her to pass as a boy. Such a description of her seems significant when we recall that her female protagonists are usually androgynous and prepubescent. As Binding's book on Lorca argues, preoccupation with androgynous characters may in and of itself be an expression of a writer's homosexuality.

Certainly, many girls who read *Harriet the Spy* as children count it as a milestone in the process whereby they discovered and accepted their sexual orientation as lesbians. Students at both of the universities where I have taught have confided that *Harriet* was important in their growing awareness and acceptance of themselves as lesbians. A lesbian colleague feels so strongly that this was the case that every year on Fitzhugh's birthday, she makes a ritual of rereading *Harriet*. Finally, there is *The Second WomanSleuth Anthology*, edited by Irene Zahava and dedicated to Harriet M. Welsch.[17] It includes stories—for example, Elizabeth Pincus's "Trouble on the Beat" and Bonnie Morris's "My Lover's Deadly Diary"—about lesbian detectives who openly acknowledge their identification with Harriet as children. Indeed, the heroine of the Pincus story says, "Harriet stole my heart when I was a kid—maybe that's what made me a dyke. Or a private eye" (Zahava, 26).

Nevertheless, *Harriet the Spy* is not a book about a lesbian, but rather one about a bright, outspoken, independent, boyish girl, who might or might not grow up to be gay. It, therefore, speaks powerfully to every reader who in one or more ways wants to be, or finds herself, a nontraditional female, as well as to those many lesbians who find it as girls (or even later) and adopt it as "their book." Childhood, not sexual orientation, was Louise Fitzhugh's primary subject, although sometime during the mid-to-late sixties, she did write a novel for young adults ("Amelia") about a childhood friend's difficulty coming to terms with her lesbianism. Unfortunately, her agent refused to represent it, and the manuscript was subsequently lost. Had it been published, however, I doubt that Fitzhugh would have been seen all that differently today. Being gay never troubled or obsessed Fitzhugh as did her repressive childhood. She was, consequently, first and foremost a children's writer. The influence of her sexual orientation on her writing is, as Martin says it usually is (Martin, 219), indirect. In her case, this is evident in her portraits of boyish girls and in her preoccupation with the horror of various forms of bigotry. Nevertheless, that she was gay explains the recurrence and force of these features of her work.

Her Death

The weekend before she died, a negative prepublication review of *Nobody's Family Is Going to Change* appeared in *Publishers Weekly*.[18] It greatly upset her, and she called Marijane Meaker to talk about it. As Meaker comments, "Who's to say if one can internalize distress to the point of causing an aneurysm?" No one really knows what causes an aneurysm, nor are there any warnings that one is possible. Medical theory suggests aneurysms are hereditary. On the other hand, some of her friends believe that Fitzhugh, then age forty-six, was having trouble with aging. Like her father, she was at times a heavy drinker. Also she did not carefully attend to her diet, and she lived with a great deal of internal stress. Combined with high blood pressure, these factors may have contributed to her death.

In any case, on Monday, because Fitzhugh had an extremely painful headache and coughed up some blood, she called an ambulance. At the hospital, she went into a coma, from which she never awakened, suffering several aneurysms in the brain. She died on 19 November 1974, ten days before the appearance of *Nobody's Family Is Going to Change.* Her death was especially eerie because ever since having a mastoid operation as a small child, she had feared brain damage. Indeed, she did several paintings of herself with her head all bandaged and one self-portrait with one side in the shadows—the side on which she had the aneurysms.

Apparently, she left many paintings and manuscripts at her death, including diaries she had kept since she was 11. Lois Morehead, her literary executor, has attempted to publish as many of the manuscripts as possible. A representative of Dell has read through all of the material left; besides her, only Mrs. Morehead has read it all, and she has stated that she will now allow access only to someone with a contract to write a full-length biography. In addition to publication of four books since Fitzhugh's death, Mrs. Morehead has approved two scripts based on *Nobody's Family Is Going to Change,* both called *The Tap Dance Kid.*[19] The first was an after-school television special in 1978, produced by Learning Corporation, and the second was a very successful Broadway production in 1983–84, which won several Tony awards. Not long ago, she approved the script and staging of *Harriet the Spy* by the Children's Theatre in Minneapolis.[20] Further publication of manuscripts left at Fitzhugh's death is also anticipated and, perhaps, other adaptations for television, film, and/or stage production.

Fitzhugh's early death and the mystery surrounding her life may account for the false rumor that she committed suicide, a rumor that invaded children's literature circles shortly after her death and still seems to prevail there. Her friends were shocked to hear this rumor and wish to put an end to it forever. The details and consistency of their accounts of Fitzhugh's death, as well as the passion and vitality of her life, convince one that her death was not a suicide.

Conclusion

Finally, regardless of missing details and inconsistencies in her friends' stories about her, an important inference about Fitzhugh as a writer for children can be made. She was a natural to enter the field of children's literature because of her lifelong need and struggle to express her own childhood's significance for her and for all children. As has been suggested, she remembered herself as an emotionally abused child, as deprived of the love and comfort she needed as a small child, as never understood. Throughout her growing up years, she felt as if she did not fit in her family or in society and as if no one appreciated her for who she was. Her defense was to view herself as an artist. All the evidence convinces one that her family pampered and indulged her, even as they refused to let her be herself. In any case, she sustained her ego sufficiently to break away and to become an artist and to succeed, although if her characters' motivation is also autobiographical, as one can reasonably assume, her ongoing battle with insecurity must have sometimes painfully motivated her own work.

Several of her friends believe that just before she died, she had finished writing children's literature and would have gone on to publish for adults. All that she published, nevertheless, was for children, and even the two manuscripts summarized earlier in this chapter are about her childhood. Her first years of life clearly preoccupied her emotionally, spiritually, and intellectually all of her adult life, and it is difficult to believe that she had transcended them at her death. The intensity of these years, reflected in her personality, are the subject of the poem James Merrill wrote for her memorial service: "Never would there be a heaven or hell, We once agreed, like those of youth." He goes on to say:

Just stick to your own story,
Humorous and heartrending and uncouth.
Its little tomboy damozel
Became the figure in our repertory
Who stood for truth.

Merrill's poem succinctly captures what much of this chapter addresses. Fitzhugh's story—her life and her books—is "humorous and heartrending and uncouth." Its hero is a nontraditional female, not yet sexual in her books but already rebelling against the restrictions and conventions of femininity and already an artist. Most important, she stands for truth—not for what others believe is or should be true, but for what she knows in the very fibre of her being. This truth is often so unexpected and individualistic, especially in *Harriet* and *The Long Secret,* that many of Fitzhugh's reviewers rejected her work as "uncouth"—that is, inappropriate and crude—and completely missed its humor and compassion. Because of her commitment to honesty, she, more than any other writer of her time, changed the nature of children's literature. She talked about subjects never before mentioned; she portrayed adults who were weak, wrong, and worse; and she told children to trust their own perceptions. Whatever else may be said of her life and her work, to say that she "stood for truth" is to identify her genius. Her passion for truth served her and us well. She told children what they had seldom or never been told, and she convinced adults that children could and should be told these truths. It is only fitting that she be remembered as the one "who stood for truth." It was her means of survival and her gift to her readers.

2

The Range of the Artist:
Pictures, Collaborations,
and Picture Books

Fitzhugh illustrated all her work but three of the four manuscripts published since her death; *Sport* lacks illustrations, and Susanna Natti and Susan Bonner, respectively, illustrated *I Am Three* and *I Am Four*. Five of her picture book texts have been published: *Suzuki Beane; Bang, Bang, You're Dead* (both with Sandra Scoppetone); and the three *I Am* books—the two already mentioned and *I Am Five*, which she did illustrate. There are several other unpublished picture book texts: *I Am Six*, which is supposed to be published by Dell, "The Owl and the Lark," which Harper agreed to publish and Mrs. Morehead withdrew,[1] and some other manuscripts Mrs. Morehead considers less finished than these. Finally, there are the illustrations for *Harriet the Spy, The Long Secret,* and *Nobody's Family Is Going to Change*.

Caricature

All of Fitzhugh's illustrations are caricature, that is, they are distortions or exaggerations of portraits, each one done in black ink or pencil and usually placed on its own blank page. Occasionally, a chair or some other background object sets the scene, but only in *Bang, Bang, You're Dead* and *The Long Secret* is there much attention to background, and in the novel, pictures of setting are usually separate from those of the characters. The focus, in other words, is on character and, more specifically, on types, which, as Edward Lucie-Smith notes, is characteristic of satiric caricature.[2]

According to Lucie-Smith, caricature ranges from the cartoon to the grotesque, that is, from slight distortion that is mildly amusing to gross exaggeration and deformity that is shocking. He also cites examples that demonstrate that the purpose of caricature is always intellectual as well as humorous and that often the "purpose is not to make us smile but to make us think" (Lucie-Smith, 9). He goes on to discuss the tragic power of some caricature. Wolfgang Kayser and Werner Hoffman also discuss caricature as existing on a continuum.[3] Hoffman, like Lucie-Smith, sees caricature as closer to the real world than the grotesque (Hoffman, 11). Kayser defines them as different in purpose. He does not see the grotesque as comic, finding it "an attempt to invoke and subdue the demonic aspects of the world" (Kayser, 182). Invoking images of the monstrous and nightmarish underworld, the grotesque exists, in Northrop Frye's terms, in the realm of tragic, dark irony.[4]

Fitzhugh's caricature exhibits the whole range of purposes. Much of it seems very close to cartoon, some offers the mild satire of a middle territory, and a little is grotesque. Indeed, in tone, her drawings often reflect her text, her range in tone resulting largely from the stock of types she depends on.

The Nontraditional Girl
The most important of these types appears, not very surprisingly, in her very first book, *Suzuki Beane*. This is the independent, nonconforming, egocentric, creative female child. Suzuki, Harriet, Jessie Mae Jenkins, the only girl in *Bang, Bang, You're Dead,* Emma, and the protagonist in *I Am Five* are all examples. Neither the figure nor face of any of these is greatly distorted. None are pretty; all appear sturdy and athletic. All but Emma and the

girl in *I Am Five* have straight hair. Emma's has a straight outline, if a curly texture, and the five-year-old's is curly but messy.
None of them is overweight but Emma, and she is not shown as
grotesquely overweight, though Fitzhugh does portray a few
characters as such. Suzuki and the girl in *Bang, Bang* also have
messy hair and clothes, and only the five-year old wears a dress.
Noses are too large to be dainty, as are mouths and hands and
feet. Eyes tend to be round and dark, suggesting the character's
innocence, honesty, and intensity. These are all positive characters, but they are not cuddly or unequivocally lovable. They are
prickly and cocky. Often, they are shown on the move. One thinks
of Harriet hanging on to a window ledge and of Suzuki dancing.
Clearly, they are all nontraditional females, and they trust themselves more than anyone else. Those who wish to receive their
trust have to earn it. In their self-absorption and egocentrism,
Fitzhugh's nontraditional girls are sometimes admirable, sometimes irritating, and always amusing. More will be said of their
personalities in the discussion of the texts.

The Nontraditional Boy

A companion for this first type is the sensitive male child, also
introduced in *Suzuki Beane* in the character of Henry Martin.
Sport and Willie are other examples. Drawn with a thinner, softer
line than their female counterparts, they often have skinny bodies and angular joints. Like those of the nontraditional girls with
whom they are friends, their eyes tend to be round and dark.
Their hair, however, widely varies. Sport's is straight and messy,
Henry's is wispy, and Willie's is tightly curled but closely cropped.
In keeping with their generally less substantial look than that of
their female friends, they have little hair. They look soft and vulnerable. Like Suzuki, Harriet, and Emma, they look like what
they are, nontraditional in their sex role behavior.

The Sensitive Girl

Another of Fitzhugh's types is the sensitive female child—most
notably Beth Ellen, but to a lesser extent Harriet's friend Janie.
Beth Ellen looks much like Henry Martin; Janie, much like Sport.

Janie is very thin, with straight, fine, messy hair. She always wears a dress. Her head seems too large for her body, and her features a bit too small for her head, her freckles and mouth dominating her face. In two pictures, she wears what Fitzhugh calls her "outrageous smile." It does indeed make her look ferocious. The heroine of *The Long Secret* is Fitzhugh's most traditional female in appearance. Rounded, small of feature and hands and feet, Beth Ellen even has curly hair. But, of course, the long secret is that her external self is not her internal one. Both Janie and Beth Ellen suffer to the extent that they conform to the female sex role. Janie, however, does so because her mother requires it, and she is always resistant, even though her resistance (her smile) shows only occasionally. Beth Ellen is in deeper trouble than Janie until the end of *The Long Secret* because she conforms out of submerged anger. It is not, therefore, surprising that Fitzhugh's drawings of Beth Ellen show her as rather thoroughly feminine. Nor is it surprising that Beth Ellen often is still and sad in appearance. Often she is lying down and completely unmoving. Her eyes most frequently look off to one side and down, making her appear pensive.

The Intellectual
The intellectual is one type of grown up whom Fitzhugh treats as sympathetically as she does the types of children thus far discussed. Ole Golly, Mr. Waldenstein, and Harriet's dad are examples. They are, of course, all very different. What drawings of them have in common is a heavier line than is used on most of the other characters in *Harriet*. They all have very dark hair, although Mr. Waldenstein has lost most of his. Both Ole Golly and Mr. Welsch have thin, large, angular bodies whereas Mr. Waldenstein is rounded. All three have very broad shoulders, but again Mr. Waldenstein's are sloping rather than straight. The eyes, noses, and mouths of all three are on the generous side, and rather than looking down at one, all three stare straight ahead, their eyes open and round. They look definite and sure of themselves and yet welcoming or open. Neither Old Golly nor Mr. Welsch seems very soft, but Mr. Waldenstein certainly does.

Ole Golly. Reprinted by permission of Harper & Row and Victor Gollancz, Ltd., from p. 23 of *Harriet the Spy*. ©1964 by Louise Fitzhugh.

Black Characters

All of Fitzhugh's black characters seem sympathetic. Besides Emma and Willie Sheridan in *Nobody's Family Is Going to Change,* who have already been mentioned as examples of other types, there is their mother, Virginia Sheridan, described in the text as a socialite, but drawn in soft charcoal to look pensive. Seated with one hand under her chin and staring off to the right, she seems thoughtful and caring. The other two black characters are the maid Helen in *Suzuki Beane* and an old black man, The Preacher, in *The Long Secret.* Both are less pretentious and more caring than most of the other adults in Fitzhugh's books. Both have large welcoming smiles, broad noses, and large, open eyes.

Helen is a large woman, whose uniform is black, covered by a large white apron. She is outlined with a thinner and softer line than is characteristic of the drawings in *Suzuki Beane.* Her face is thinly lined to look charcoal, indicating her color. In the second picture of her, we see only the back of her unfilled upper torso and head, as she envelops Suzuki in a big hug.

There are also two pictures of The Preacher, one from the front and the other from the back. Very thin and dark and heavily lined, he looks old and strange. His clothes are almost entirely pure black, including a hat. By way of contrast, his very dark skin is lighter than his clothes and draws our attention, especially since there is a touch of white at his throat, in his eyes, and in his nails. The contrast in value focuses us on his smiling, open-eyed face, on the sloping shoulders, and on his hands leaning on a cane. His eyes seem to be looking up, which reinforces one's sense of him as a small man as does the blank space above and below him on the page. Like Fitzhugh's artists, he is less a type, a representative of a class, than an eccentric, a deviation from the norm. Like her other black characters, he is kind. Like Helen, he seems to understand children more fully and sympathetically than most other adults do, especially when the children are socially unconventional. But as extensive use of black usually indicates in Fitzhugh's drawings, there is more substance to The Preacher than there is to most people, and as his highly unusual appearance indicates, he is one of a kind. Indeed, he is so different and dramatic in his appearance that one might at first see him as Harriet does—as the villain. As a result of the long talk Harriet, Beth Ellen, and Jessie Mae have with him in chapter 21, however, we, like them, begin to perceive his mystery, after which we see him leave, now practically all black and much smaller than in the first picture of him.

The Artist

The artist is yet a sixth type in Fitzhugh's drawings, created using a technique very similar to that used to portray the sensitive child. Examples are Suzuki's parents and the poet at Henry Martin's house in *Suzuki Beane,* Harrison Withers and Miss Berry in *Harriet the Spy,* Bunny in *The Long Secret,* and Dipsey Bates in *Nobody's Family Is Going to Change.* No matter how respected, all of these characters receive funny portraits, although the tone of the humor differs.

The heavy line on Suzuki's parents, their messy hair, sunken dark eyes that look down—all reveal that they take themselves too seriously, as the text makes plain when they reject Suzuki's friendship with Henry. Fitzhugh makes fun of their narrow-mindedness by giving them such stiff bodies and rigid attitudes. Here she shows in her drawings that it is not being different that counts, but being who one is. In rejecting Henry as a representative of the artificial rich, they judge him by appearances, just as they are judged by society. The point clearly is that they are as artificial as Henry's parents—in a heavier, but no less pretentious way.

The poet at Henry's house, Fitzhugh's satire of young James Merrill, is their opposite.[5] He looks like a boy. Thin, soft, and posed, he is definitely artificial. Every hair on his head is carefully in place; his collar is high and closed; his tie, thin; his vest, decorated with tiny flowers. One small hand holds the poem he reads; the other, a pair of dark-rimmed, circular glasses. Whereas the Beanes fill the page with dark, heavy lines, the page portraying him is mostly white.

Another important difference is that the line that creates him is carefully controlled in contrast to the more haphazard line for the Beanes. They seem to have more substance but less control, and he, the reverse.

A thin, wispy, spontaneous line creates both the artists in *Harriet*. Harrison Withers looks like a much softened and older version of the poet in *Suzuki Beane*. He is thinner and drawn in a thinner line. There are more lines to him, and they are broken and repeated. The effect is to make him look removed from the here and now—dreamy and vulnerable and caring. He seems just as self-absorbed as the poet, but less pretentious and more likeable. The technique used to create the other artist, Miss Berry, Harriet's dancing teacher at school, is even more wispy. Here again is another extreme artists may illustrate. Miss Berry is not rigid, but she is as pretentious as the poet in *Suzuki*. Forgetting her audience, she loses herself in her imagination of the drama the children will reenact in their dance. She is as insubstantial because of the wispy lines that characterize her as the poet is in the carefully controlled line that defines him and leaves most of the page blank. The pretentions of each are thus contrastingly revealed, the one well-defined by a simple line that is unfilled, the other left undefined by an overabundance of line that goes every which way.

The portrait of Bunny, the piano player that Beth Ellen has a crush on in *The Long Secret* and whom we eventually discover is sponsored and pursued by Agatha Plummer, is similar to those of the poet, Harrison Withers, and Miss Berry. Drawn in a thin, broken, repeated line, he is, nevertheless, neither as wispy as Miss Berry nor as full as Harrison Withers. Similar to the poet, he stands on a mostly blank page, with very little line required to define him. Only one line defines his facial outline, only two his legs, and only three or four his shirt. He is another artist who lacks substance.

Finally, there is Dipsey Bates in *Nobody's Family Is Going to Change*, a grown-up version of his nephew Willie. His body is the same thin, fluid shape as Willie's, only more so. The hair and eyes are the same, too, although the mouth and grin are even fuller. The full coat and bell-bottom pants accentuate the motion of his body. He is every inch a dancer. Like Harrison Withers, his figure and face have substance, for in the drawings in *Nobody's Family Is Going to Change* Fitzhugh uses soft, rubbed pencil, rather than simple line drawings. The resulting light and dark areas give

body to the shapes of each of the five main characters, whose portraits are featured at the book's beginning. Also similar here to
the image of Harrison is Dipsey's softness. He seems vulnerable
and self-absorbed. He also seems joyful. But one would suspect
from the drawing that he would not be much help to Willie in his
struggle with his father. Inspiration, mostly in the form of a role
model, is the most help he has to offer.

Despite the variety of technique in the creation of Fitzhugh's
artists, they are all eccentrics. The numerous and differing
examples of this type indicate her fascination with and her
amusement at artists. All are delightfully funny, but some, if fascinating, are less admirable than others. Those laughed at most
are the ones who display their eccentricity as a pose. Clearly, they
are fakes, using their roles as artists to feel superior rather than
genuinely to express who they are.

The Socialite
Another type very common in Fitzhugh's illustrations, and also
an example of the fake, is the socialite. Examples are Henry's parents in *Suzuki Beane,* Angela Plummer in *Harriet the Spy* and
The Long Secret, and Beth Ellen's parents in *The Long Secret.* The
two sets of parents are very similarly drawn. On the women a
very thin and minimal outline suggests the hair, nose, and face.
The emphasis is on the eyes and mouth of both mothers. Henry's
mother's eyes are heavily outlined in black as are her eyebrows.
The irises are toward the top of heavily slanted eyes, making her
seem to be looking down. The rather large mouth is open, and the
teeth are clenched. The effect is a bored, superior grimace. Beth
Ellen's mother wears black sunglasses, and her mouth is closed,
but she looks similarly distant and aloof. The husbands are
drawn in much the same fashion. The line is a bit thicker, the
nose more pronounced, and the hair and face more defined than
is the case for their wives. Both husbands' mouths are closed
tightly in straight lines, and the eyes are a bit darker than the
rest of the head. One notices Henry's father, like Beth Ellen's
mother, because of heavy black at the eyes, in this case, an eye
patch on one eye calling attention to the thin eye not covered. The

Beth Ellen's parents. Reprinted by permission of Harper & Row and Victor Gollancz, Ltd., from p. 248 of *The Long Secret*. ©1965 by Louise Fitzhugh.

hands of both men, like their whole bodies, seem posed. Insubstantial like some of Fitzhugh's artists, indeed even more so, they are nevertheless more unpleasant because they are more unnerving. Flat in effect, clearly isolated from everyone else, bloodless and bodiless, they seem capable of any atrocity, which, of course, the texts confirm.

The Bully
Another negative type is the bully. Examples are the teachers in *Suzuki Beane* and William Sheridan. Suzuki's school teacher, Miss Shoemaker, is large-headed, thin-necked, many-lined, and plump. The line is relatively heavy on her, although less so than for the Beanes. Her hair is in a fairly tight bun, and her nose is quite large and pointed. Her eyes are hidden behind small glasses, and her mouth is straight and sunken. Henry's dancing teacher, Miss Caroline Perfect, is quite similar. She is skinny and drawn with a finer line. We see her from the front, not the side. Also she does not wear glasses, and her mouth is slightly open. Despite these differences, both teachers are stereotypically old maids, which perhaps explains their rigidity and their need to bully. Mr. Sheridan is drawn quite differently, though he similarly fills the page. Done in a soft charcoal, his three-piece suit and tie connote wealth, but his head and body are round and look soft. His eyes are open and round. Only his clenched lips reveal any rigidity, and perhaps the position of his hands, one behind his head and the other on one hip. One feels more sympathy, in fact, for the man in this drawing than for the man in the story. His soft eyes seem sad; he looks sincere. One might suspect he is more mistaken than rigid.

The Fat Person
For many, a very troublesome type in Fitzhugh's work is the fat person. One suspects that her drawings of fat people reflect an obsession with physical deformity, rather than with the rigidities of personality. For many of us, it is uncomfortable to laugh at the physically abnormal purely for its own sake, especially if there is no compassion or understanding of the person offered in the text.

Perhaps Fitzhugh's negativity about and obsession with fat had their origin in her perception of her uncle's and her maternal grandmother's obesity.

In any case, her grotesque portrait of Ole Golly's mom in *Harriet the Spy* distresses many viewers, although surely even the most disapproving must suppress a smile or giggle. It is a funny picture. Lumpy, with both arms and legs hanging outward, her large, undefined body occupies the middle of the page. She faces straight out, her large, round eyes vacant, except for a small dot of ink, her mouth hanging open, her hair looking matted and uncombed. The combination of huge, shapeless, white sweater, flowered dress, and long, black boots completes the picture. From the text we know she is simpleminded, but the presentation of her there, too, is without sympathy.

Mama Jenkins and her son Norman are more important in *The Long Secret* than is Ole Golly's mom in *Harriet the Spy*. Perhaps that is why they become more sympathetic characters than Ole Golly's mom. In any case, Fitzhugh's drawings of them are just as outrageously funny. Norman's large, round belly makes his head seem small by comparison. His face displays a small patch of freckles under tiny eyes and over a tiny nose and mouth. His black hair, his black shorts tucked up in his crotch, and his huge black tennis shoes, as well as his long, skinny legs and small head, accentuate his large belly in its white T-shirt. Mama Jenkins has similar black hair, but there is more of it, and it is more matted in appearance. She looks much like her son, but she smiles, her body is huge, and black dominates the drawing of her. Her hair and the softly draped dress she wears are almost entirely black. Only a huge arm and her face, except for the bit of line that defines her small features and her freckles, are white. Her young daughter Magnolia sits on her shoulders, a thin replica in white of her mother. Both look pleasant and happy, if bizarre.

Emma in *Nobody's Family Is Going to Change,* yet another fat character, is less weird looking than these three. Certainly, she is one of a kind with her triangular hair and her soft, doughy body, but she is neither as huge nor as distorted in other ways as the other three are. One could certainly conclude that Fitzhugh's understanding of Emma's weight problem, as revealed in the text, makes Fitzhugh less interested here in laughing at fatness as a physical deformity than had been the case before.

Weird Little Kids

There is much evidence that Fitzhugh's caricatures are as much the result of a fascination with the physically unusual as of a desire to satirize moral rigidity. In addition to the fat threesome just described, weird little kids of all shapes abound in her books—Suzuki's classmates, Harriet's classmates, Little Joe Curry, Magnolia Jenkins, and all the boys in *Bang, Bang, You're Dead!*

Because they are the most extreme examples, the latter deserve some special attention. Alixe Gordin revealed that the seven boys and one girl (already discussed) who appear in *Bang, Bang, You're Dead!* are all caricatures of some of Fitzhugh's adult friends. Still done with pen and ink, they also frequently rely on cross-hatching so that the figures all have more body than those in the early books, but are harder than those in *Nobody's Family* because they are drawn with ink rather than charcoal. The background, incongruously, is only outlined and two dimensional in contrast with the figures—with one exception. In the scene where James and his army vow to "fight to the end!" the club house and its furniture are crosshatched, and the floor is smudged, nearly solid black. This scene is somewhat ominous in contrast with the blank white space of the others, but the change in mood seems insufficient reason for a radical, one-time change in technique. Indeed, the attempt to present setting throughout the book is a failure, only emphasizing that Fitzhugh's real interest in her illustrations, as in her writing, is in character.

As is evident in Fitzhugh's very choice of caricature and satire as techniques, this interest in character is in the strange, bizarre, eccentric, or grotesque. Like her drawings of fat people and children such as Rachel Hennessey in *Harriet the Spy,* the illustrations in *Bang, Bang, You're Dead!* veer toward the grotesque. The bodies of the children are all within the normal range, from tall to short, thin to stocky. But their costumes are strange. A cone-

Cover of *Bang, Bang, You're Dead!* Reprinted by permission of Harper & Row and Victor Gollancz, Ltd., from *Bang, Bang, You're Dead!* by Louise Fitzhugh and Sandra Scoppettone. Illustrations ©1969 by Louise Fitzhugh.

shaped hat and an old military coat with epaulets adorn a slim, tall blond. A short boy with a full head of blond straight hair, parted on the side, wears a vest and cowboy boots. Another with dark hair wears an army fatigue hat. James, the leader of the first army, always stands out in his elaborate Indian headdress. Big Mike, the leader of the other army, is all in black and has a hat shaped like a police officer's. One little boy is in overalls and carries a spear, and the last is dressed in a sailor suit, its whiteness contrasting with the darkness of the others' clothes and with the black of his large, round glasses and his tie. In addition to its being interesting in and of itself, the children's bizarre garb differentiates them from one another. It also emphasizes that they are involved in play—where people dress up. So do their smiling faces.

As play becomes real fighting, the headgear gets left behind along with the smiles. As throwing rocks gives way to beating with sticks and gouging eyes, the children look more and more like each other. On each of the five pages that end the book, we see all eight injured children with hats and glasses and spears and other sharply distinguishing features missing or played down. The focus here is on blood and pain. In the first two pages, dark black flows from noses, heads, arms, and legs. Bodies are sprawled on the ground, bent, curled up, distorted with pain. In the last three, the figures all slowly rise and walk off toward the right. In the very last, they have their arms around one another as they agree never to fight again, but instead to play "Bang, Bang, You're Dead!" Here, especially, their physical differences are minimized, their bodies merging to form a harmonious whole. Once again, despite their bloody wounds, they smile. The picture recalls an earlier one, when after playing, James and his army came down the hill to eat ice cream.

The pictures in the last half of this book are without humor, surely part of the reason why this book has been negatively received by many. Fitzhugh's purpose is serious here; she wants to show how painful and ugly war really is. The children's "ferocious figures," noted by the reviewer in *The Bulletin for the Center for Children's Books* and "the gushing blood," focused on by the re-

Children lying down. Reprinted by permission of Harper & Row and Victor Gollancz, Ltd., from p. 28 of *Bang, Bang, You're Dead!* by Louise Fitzhugh and Sandra Scoppettone. Illustrations ©1969 by Louise Fitzhugh.

viewer in *Library Journal,* led reviewers such as the one in *Teacher* to use words such as "chilling" and "shocking" to describe the book.[6] For some adults, the next step after such judgments has been to reject *Bang, Bang, You're Dead!* as a children's book or at least as a picture book. Many libraries shelve it with Fitzhugh's novels, rather than with the picture books, if, indeed, it is even owned by the library. Popular sentiment, in other words, seems to judge grotesque images as inappropriate for children, although there is opinion to the contrary. All the reviews already cited praise the book's illustrations, even while they label them inappropriate for children. In any case, these are images that haunt one and speak meaningfully of the horror of violence. Particularly eloquent are Fitzhugh's pictorial recognition of the loss of individuality inevitable in violence and her celebration of the bizarre and eccentric as hallmarks of individuality.

Fitzhugh as an Illustrator

Were her gift as a caricaturist recognized, Fitzhugh's talent as an illustrator would be more appreciated. Always she shows us the eccentric or the misfit. To the extent that she values this character, there is little physical distortion in her drawing. The reverse is also true, and at her most negative, she presents us with grotesque images. Her penchant for the bizarre may never be understood because it makes us uncomfortable. It is hard to value what startles, shocks, and repulses us. It was Fitzhugh's gift always to be fascinated by such images. Children, intellectuals, blacks, artists, socialites, bullies, the fat, and the violent gave her the material for a gallery of the different and the strange—even the repulsive. The merit of this gallery for the perceptive is that almost never is an image without moral significance. Ole Golly's fat mom may be an exception, but even here one could argue that the emptiness of her life except for food is the point. With sure strokes of her pen or pencil, Fitzhugh judges each of her gallery, always elevating what is honestly individual as essential to life and condemning whatever cripples or distorts the essential. What is amazing about her art is that she never simplistically evaluates her characters. Always she enjoys their eccentricities—if only because they are funny. Often she celebrates them as hallmarks of real individuality, at other times she satirizes them, and only when distortions become grotesque, endangering the individual, does she condemn.

Picture Book Texts

Unfortunately, Fitzhugh's picture book texts are not as complex as her illustrations. The three *I Am* books are geared to very young children, *Bang, Bang, You're Dead* is very simplistic, and although suggestive of much that Fitzhugh was to explore in her novels, *Suzuki Beane* is finally too obvious and thin in its structure and implications. Their failures reflect a simplistic reliance upon types, a failure she avoided in her pictures chiefly because the visual effect of a caricaturist's techniques is always humor as well as judgment.

The *I Am* Books

I Am Three, I Am Four, and *I Am Five* belong to a genre of simple books for the beginning listener. Their lack of complexity, therefore, warrants less concern than that of Fitzhugh's other picture books. Each of them is simply a list of things a child of three, four, or five likes to and can do. As a series, they show a progression in cognitive, physical, emotional, and social development. But what is really interesting about them is their celebration of "I."

One can easily believe that the natural and thorough-going egocentricity of the preschool child would capture Louise Fitzhugh's attention. The child of three, four, or five has an uncensored tongue and a total absorption in herself. She says what she hates—food that touches other food, that new baby brother, sometimes her dog, teeth, bedtime, all those starving people, and at times everybody. She says what she likes—talking, hugs, presents, being looked at by everybody, eating only rice for two weeks, drawing, dancing, stories, and laughing. She also identifies her fears—fire engines, the dark, being little, and feeling "like a fat silly"—and her vanity—showing off her bathing suit or snowsuit—and her vitality—talking, dancing, and drawing on and on and on, "running away with myself" until "I think I am not going to be able to stop"—and her stubbornness— "sometimes I refuse to be moved." The point is that she is what she is with no pretense.

Obviously, Fitzhugh would approve. Indeed, in their celebration of egocentricity, these little books present one variation on Fitzhugh's major theme. Here she shows clearly that we all come into the world sure of what pleases and displeases us and liking ourselves. As the series progresses, there is increased negative feeling, including a slight lessening of self-esteem. Strongly suggested is that the child learns through encounters with others and the world to abandon her egocentricity—not always to her benefit. Still the stress in these texts is on "I am."

Bang, Bang, You're Dead!

Although very simple, the texts of the three *I Am* books are more successful than that of *Bang, Bang, You're Dead!* written by Fitzhugh and Sandra Scoppetone. Whereas the general public seems to have been most discomfited by the book's graphic illustrations of violence, the reviewers largely objected to its message-dominated text. The *Bulletin of the Center for Children's Books* concludes, "The treatment is insubstantial, the message worthy, and the story not as original as one might expect from the innovative Miss Fitzhugh" (174). *The Library Journal* faults the book for being obvious melodrama "pawned for the anti-war moral" (2496). *Publishers Weekly* says, "She has a message—the futility of war. And a message can be synonymous with disaster—too often it transforms a fine writer into a truculent reformer."[7] These evaluations of the text are correct; its two-part structure and its theme are obvious and predictable. We all know that playing at war can be joyful and that real fighting is destructive and painful. We know as soon as the second group of four children appears and the fight is assured how the book will end. Also the language is simple and uninspired. Only the pictures lift this book above the pedestrian. Only they exhibit any originality and vitality.

Suzuki Beane

The text of *Suzuki Beane* is more interesting than that of *Bang, Bang, You're Dead!* Although it is attributed to Sandra Scoppetone, Alixe Gordin says the text was written in collaboration with Fitzhugh. The book is mostly unknown and difficult to locate these days. As Nodelman first noted, it is so rooted in the language and people of the late fifties that it is dated (Nodelman, 134). Suzuki's parents, as her name might suggest, are beatniks, and their conversation is full of "like," "man," "dig," and "swings." Most children today have never heard of beatniks and would find the language a barrier to understanding. But the barrier would not be insurmountable if the book offered something else that the contemporary child found valuable. *Harriet the Spy* is dated in some of its details, for example, the price of egg creams and a child's being free to wander the East Side of New York City alone. But children still hungrily devour it. It is not the beatniks or their language that accounts for *Suzuki Beane*'s failure to survive. It is rather the authors' lack of control of their materials.

For the student of Fitzhugh's development, this book, her first picture book, is fascinating because so much of what was to come is there in utero. It is a book about real and fake art and artists. It satirizes the rich, the authoritarian, and the pretentious. It portrays a strong, nontraditional girl as a heroine. It reveals her strong dependency needs even as it celebrates her independence. It savagely attacks parents for failing to understand and validate their children's feelings, and it tells children that they are people, too, and deserve to be treated as such by their parents. The conclusion of the book also rings familiar. Suzuki and Henry take matters into their own hands, as Fitzhugh's child characters inevitably do, the message being that parents will not or cannot take care of their children and that the children must, therefore, do so themselves or deny who they are as individuals and live as their parents wish.

Here is the substance of all of Fitzhugh's later work, but not meaningfully or movingly developed and ordered. It reads like a series of quick shots, almost as if Scoppetone and Fitzhugh had to get in everything that irritated them. They laugh at most of what they write about—beatniks, conformist children, school-teachers, dancing school, socialites, elitist poets, and cartoons. But besides laughing (with Suzuki as their mouthpiece), they approve of the beatniks' relaxed life-style and commitment to freedom, relationships, and creativity, and, most important, they tell the serious story of Suzuki's and Henry's disillusionment with their parents. While becoming friends, Henry and Suzuki each confront the other's parents as representatives of a rejected, ridiculed life-style. That both sets of parents fail to see the children as people reveals how thoroughly they are controlled by ideas, rather than by feelings. They are closed off from anyone who might threaten their perception of reality—even their children. So the two children run away.

So much here is contradictory or troublesome. How are we to understand Suzuki's being able to value Henry when her parents are not able to? Presumably they taught her to be who she is. In her moving response to Helen's hug and in her brashness with her classmates, we see her need for and awkwardness about acceptance and affection.[8] Her fear of subways and those parts of the city she's never visited also suggests that she is a little girl much in need of parenting. Both suggest that her parents are probably quite selfish and not very loving—that their words about how life ought to be lived are mostly just words. But if these suggestions about them are true, how did she learn to be different? Throughout most of the book, Suzuki is, in fact, very much their child and a marvelous vehicle for criticism of those who conform or pretend. But her role in the first half of the book conflicts with the one she performs in the last half. They don't go together to form a whole. The story breaks in half. First, it satirizes society from a beatnik point of view, and second, it reveals Suzuki's perceiving and rejecting her beatnik parents for what they are. Unrealistically, it also shows her as unafraid and happy to run away. If afraid of a subway, she would certainly be terrified of "going on the road."

With character development, elimination of some parts, and revision of the ending, *Suzuki Beane* might have succeeded. But as it stands, it is bits and pieces of many things and never finally one thing. It is a first step, valuable because it has greater substance than the *I Am* books and because message does not entirely dominate story as it does in *Bang, Bang, You're Dead!*. Indeed, it suggests much about what was to come in Fitzhugh's best novels, where she conveys the complexity, power, and wholeness characteristic of her best illustrations.

Harriet at the window. Reprinted by permission of Harper & Row and Victor Gollancz, Ltd., from p. 55 of *Harriet the Spy*. ©1964 by Louise Fitzhugh.

3

Portrait of the Artist as a Girl: *Harriet the Spy*

The genius of *Harriet the Spy* is that it explores the experiences of an outsider content to be one. It both celebrates and critiques Harriet's personality and the environment that produced her. Fitzhugh portrays Harriet as a thoroughgoing eccentric. In light of her inevitable career as an artist, Harriet's self-absorption and her fascination with her own mind take on additional meaning. Fitzhugh sets the stage for a complex and moving exploration of the artist as necessarily both selfish and lonely, of the outsider as potentially both a threat to and a benefactor of society, of the nontraditional female as displaying more self-esteem but less empathy than the traditional female, of the child nurtured intellectually but not emotionally, and of much more. *Harriet the Spy* is a book rich in emotional and intellectual power. And all of its power arises from Fitzhugh's discovery and understanding of Harriet M. Welsch, the outsider *par excellence*.

The Critics

To evaluate the significance of *Harriet the Spy*, one must, therefore, understand and appreciate its heroine, as all too often readers have failed to do. Its first reviewers were, unfortunately, often off the mark, which accounts for the book's never having won an award given by adults. The *Book Week* review calls Harriet "precocious, intense, egocentric and mean," the one in the *Christian Science Monitor* speaks of "rather a pathetic figure—too pathetic, one hopes, for young people to admire," and Ruth Hill Viguers in *Horn Book* settles for "disagreeable" as a description for all the book's characters.[1] Even 10 years later, the review in the *Times Literary Supplement,* although essentially favorable, judges Harriet's suffering in the middle of the book as evidence that her spying "has got out of hand,"[2] and Francis Molson in "Another Look at *Harriet the Spy*" sees her not as self-absorbed and egocentric, but rather as "groping towards self-acceptance and respect."[3]

The most recent studies of the book also make errors in their judgment of Harriet. Perry Nodelman describes her as an arrogant observer who lacks respect for other people (Nodelman, 136–37); Hamida Bosmajian sees her as coping "with her isolation by connecting herself mechanically through routines" and as trying "to control the world through her notebook";[4] and Lissa Paul calls her a feminist writer.[5]

To be fair, these lengthy studies of the novel have all increased understanding of Harriet. But each in its special focus has illuminated only one portion of her personality. Molson's interest is in the development of the writer, which he sees as requiring enormous self-esteem. I contend that Harriet already loves herself before the novel begins and that what she learns is not self-acceptance but empathy or increased understanding and, therefore, acceptance of others.[6] But what Molson says about Harriet's using her writing to understand the world is correct and explains what reviewers have seldom understood. She is not "mean"; she does not intend that anyone see her notebook. She writes for herself.

Nodelman's and Bosmajian's analyses of the novel are giant leaps forward. Still Nodelman's perception of Harriet as arrogant and lacking respect requires qualification. Harriet does not know she is either. The degree to which Harriet is innocent, that is, ignorant of how others might perceive her, especially as she reveals herself in her notebook comments, has too often been missed by her critics. She is merely being honest about what she sees and thinks and would be startled to learn she is judged "arrogant." Bosmajian's insightful psychological and philosophical reading of the novel goes beyond Nodelman's breakthrough identification of *Harriet the Spy* as satire to show that the novel "meshes two modes of fiction—satire and psychological realism" (Bosmajian, 73). Bosmajian comes closer than any other critic to seeing truly that Harriet is a heroine, recognizing "her indomitable spirit that refuses to turn destructively against her self" (Bosmajian, 81). But rather than stress Harriet's strengths, Bosmajian focuses on the difficulties life poses for Harriet—the disconnectedness (the nonsense) that characterizes Harriet's life on the psychological, social, and metaphysical levels.

Her analysis stresses the struggling, troubled Harriet and not the intensely alive and vibrant Harriet, who is also there in Fitzhugh's novel. It is true that Harriet's routines grant her the psychological security that her environment does not provide and that she writes in her notebook in order to possess what she sees, that is, to remember, analyze, and understand the life she observes. Routines and notebooks are techniques used by many creative people to impose discipline and order on fertile imaginations and intense sensibilities that might otherwise prove confusing and overwhelming. As such, they are a means of survival and psychological health. They create the space and distance—the control—necessary for creativity. It is only when they become the end rather than the means that such techniques are psychologically destructive—only when they are an attempt to control life rather than a means of self-expression.

Lissa Paul's "The Feminist Writer as Heroine in *Harriet the Spy*" celebrates Harriet as a trickster figure, both successful and subversive. In Paul's words, such a heroine appears "conforming and obedient, while at the same time remaining true to herself, her life, and her art" (Paul, 70). She thus "gets away with lying, gossiping, and with generally being rude" (Paul, 72). This reading of *Harriet* is certainly correct, but again, partial—denying the price Harriet pays for being herself, attributing motivation to her that she never consciously realizes, and needing the corrective of Bosmajian's reading. Breaking free of stereotypes about women and girls and revealing the dangers of individualism, Fitzhugh is a feminist writer. Harriet is at best only beginning to become one.

Harriet's Personality

Incorrect, partial, or insufficiently qualified as these analyses of Harriet may be, they establish the depth and fullness of Fitzhugh's characterization. For readers of *Harriet the Spy*, its heroine exists as if she were a real person, as in a way she was. She was perhaps based on several people, including Louise Fitzhugh. In *Me Me Me Me Me*, M. E. Kerr's autobiographical account of adolescence, there is a chapter called "Marijane the Spy."[7] Marijane Meaker is M. E. Kerr's real name. "Marijane the Spy" is the story of 11-year-old Marijane's spying on and persecution of Millicent, a young girl who came to live in Marijane's hometown to be near her father, a convict at the local prison. Before she gets into the story proper, Kerr tells us of her window peeping as a child, of her brother's hanging a sign saying "Marijane the Spy" on her door, and of her listening to everything her mother—a great gossip—said on the phone. There are obvious parallels in Fitzhugh's novel: the name on the sign, window peeping, and listening to her mother's gossip (Harriet, of course, listens to everyone's). The story and novel are also similar in their concerns with innocence, arrogance, and insensitivity. Kerr tells us what she learned: "I think the experience with Millicent started me focusing in a little on the underdog. I think I felt my first real shame at how I'd treated someone, and I know that [in my writing for young adults,] I . . . try to point out that prejudice of any kind is wrong, that winning and losing in life isn't everything" (Kerr, 58).

Relating that she had told her friend, Louise Fitzhugh, about her childhood experience, Kerr also establishes an explicit connection between *Harriet the Spy* and "Marijane the Spy": "We used to swap stories and discuss ideas, and when she wrote her first book for young people, called *Harriet the Spy*, I said, "Hey, wait a minute! That's my story! I told you I was Marijane the Spy, and you stole that idea from me! Louise said all kids are spies when they're little. She was and I was . . . and she just beat me to the punch and told the story first" (Kerr, 58).

Although Fitzhugh may have taken from Meaker the idea of spying and something of her character at 11, Alixe Gordin points out that she also took ideas for Harriet from other sources. For example, Harriet's spy outfit is exactly the favorite play clothes worn as a child by another friend, Betty Beard, a California writer and actress. Fitzhugh undoubtedly used a variety of sources, including her own childhood. The result was that she complexly explored and universalized the idea of a child's spying.

Unlike Marijane, Harriet never experiences shame, but then her motive for spying is not to gain power over or to torment others, but to gain knowledge of how others live so that she will "KNOW WHAT WAY I WANT TO LIVE AND NOT JUST LIVE LIKE MY FAMILY" (*Harriet*, 32). Following Ole Golly's advice to "SEE EVERY WAY I CAN" (*Harriet*, 32), she becomes a spy, for how else is a child, especially in our disconnected society, to learn about the lives of many adults except by listening in on their conversations and by watching them secretly at every opportunity that presents itself. As Harriet knows very well, Ole Golly does not approve of window peeping and listening at corners. She has taught Harriet the importance of privacy. She doesn't let Harriet invade hers, and she respects Harriet's. At one point in the novel, she prevents Harriet's listening to her father's explosive response to a high-stress day. Clearly, she would not approve of Harriet's spy route, as Harriet certainly knows. But inventive and curious as Harriet is, she comes up with spying as a way of getting the information she requires.

Marijane Meaker and Louise Fitzhugh as girls undoubtedly shared the intelligence, imagination, curiosity, creativity, and vitality that characterize Harriet. To a large extent, we can believe that these traits are a child's genetic inheritance—a matter of inclination and temperament. They are, furthermore, those necessary for a writer, and it is as such that Fitzhugh celebrates them in Harriet. To become a writer, a child needs to see, contemplate, understand, and remember many people engaged in many events in many different places. To observe life and to record it in a notebook are the fundamental processes involved. What's more, what one records must be what one honestly thinks and not what is nice or what one should say. The more unfettered the mind, the more likely original and honest perceptions are. Thus, even as Fitzhugh uses Harriet's notebook to reveal her limitations, she relishes Harriet's honest, critical, totally egocentric observations of others and often uses them as apt judgments of characters.

Satirized Characters

In her honest and earnest—if innocent—attempt to find out about life and herself, Harriet is a fairly adequate measure for all of the other characters, many of whom have settled for meaningless and disconnected lives. All of her classmates but her friends, Janie and Sport, and shy Beth Ellen Hanson, whom Harriet can't figure out, are, in Harriet's opinion, boring conformists and followers. Rather than seek and nourish their potential as individuals, Marion Hawthorne, Rachel Hennessey, Carrie Andrews, and Laura Peters will grow up to live just like their mothers; Pinky Whitehead and the boy with the purple socks, just like their fathers. Along her spy route, Harriet observes other examples of limited or failed lives. Again out of fear and/or ignorance, adults settle for the safe and sure rather than risk love and loss. The Dei Santis don't understand why Fabio needs the truck or in any way must differ from his older brother Bruno, who, like Mama and Papa, lives his whole life for the store. Rich Mrs. Agatha Plumber takes to her bed and thereby avoids life. The Robinsons reduce life to buying and displaying possessions; their "perfect lives" allow for total control and—consequently—complete sterility. They have walled out the possibility of intimacy with or genuine caring for another human being. They never even talk when alone.

Favored Characters

The one person on her route toward whom Harriet feels mostly positive is Harrison Withers, their shared initials revealing their connection. Harrison is an artist, who loves his work and his cats. He and Fabio are the only people Harriet spies on who have and pursue an individual passion in life, and Harrison is the only one with whom she identifies. But his seemingly total isolation from all human contact troubles her, introducing what all students of the *Künstlerroman* see as a major conflict for all artists—that between living and creating, between relationships and art (Beebe, 21–64 and Huf, 5–14). Perceptively, Bosmajian identifies Harrison as "an objective correlative for her [Harriet's] tensions," noting that "Harriet would 'wither' if she were to imitate him" (Bosmajian, 78). Linda Huf emphasizes this conflict as looming especially large in lives of female artists because their conditioning leads them to value others over themselves, and relationships over work (Huf, 5–14). In any case, Harriet is aware that she differs from Harrison in as many ways as she resembles him, even while she worries about his (her) being alone.

Clearly, Harriet also admires Sport and Janie and by the end of the novel, to some extent, Beth Ellen. Ole Golly and her boyfriend, Mr. Waldenstein, and Dr. Wagner, the psychiatrist Harriet's parents take her to visit at the end of the novel, are role models, as to some extent is her father (based on Alixe Gordin, who was also in the television business and is temperamentally very similar). It is not, in other words, that Harriet is unloving or uncaring, but rather that at a remarkably early age, she knows whom she values and why. Always these are people who, like her, are unique individuals—eccentrics. They are all to some extent loners and outsiders, both because they enjoy and require time for understanding, expressing, and developing themselves as individuals and because there are few people like them. Finally, they are, like Harriet, intelligent. They rely heavily on the mind rather than the emotions. Putting distance between them and the world, intelligence largely defines each of them.

Surely such understanding of Harriet and those she cares for came from Fitzhugh's understanding of herself and her many artist friends—and perhaps her "out" gay friends. Outrageously eccentric herself, she enjoyed flamboyant and creative self-expression, but was also angered by the way others less enamored of themselves feared and disliked such display. The key to much of her work is her distress, which most often is expressed as biting satire of conformity, with such responses to the unusual. But in *Harriet the Spy*, she also celebrates what she cherished in people—their capacity to be unique, surprising, and fascinating, and—at their best—their capacity for self-knowledge and self-expression that deepens and widens our understanding of the human condition.

Ole Golly

The source of Harriet's desire to discover and be herself is Ole Golly. As Harriet tells us, "OLE GOLLY SAYS THERE IS AS MANY WAYS TO LIVE AS THERE ARE PEOPLE ON THE EARTH AND I SHOULDN'T GO AROUND WITH BLINDERS BUT SHOULD SEE EVERY WAY I CAN. THEN I'LL KNOW WHAT WAY I WANT TO LIVE AND NOT JUST LIVE LIKE MY FAMILY" (*Harriet*, 32).

It is, of course, not merely Ole Golly's advice, but rather their relationship that nurtures Harriet's eccentric individualism. Ole Golly is Harriet's spiritual and emotional mother. She is also the mother Ole Golly herself (and Louise Fitzhugh) never had but desperately needed. The visit to Ole Golly's mother early in the book is not gratuitous satire of fat, uninvolved people, as some readers have suggested. It rather provides the background information necessary to our understanding Ole Golly and her role as Harriet's surrogate mother. As a parent, Ole Golly encourages awareness of life's variety and possibilities. She teaches Harriet to choose what she likes best rather than blindly to accept whatever happens to come along. She teaches her to avoid a life of pure routine. And she teaches her to believe that such choice is possible by providing her with an example of someone who made exactly such a choice—herself.

In other words, knowing full well the despair of not being understood and of not having one's potential nourished, she gives Harriet exactly the opposite of what her mother gave her as a child. She demonstrates that one need not grow up to be like one's family. She loves and understands Harriet for who she is, not requiring that Harriet be like her, and Harriet responds as would any child to such a mother. She listens to and respects Ole Golly, and she tries to live as Ole Golly suggests. She attempts to find out who she is and how she wants to live.

Ole Golly, writes Marijane Meaker, "sounds very much like my old friend [Fitzhugh]." Psychologically, seeing Ole Golly as the adult Louise Fitzhugh, now capable of nurturing the child Louise, makes a great deal of sense. But I also suspect that Ursula Nordstrom, Fitzhugh's editor for her first two novels, may have been a source for Ole Golly. As Charlotte Zolotow remembers, *Harriet the Spy* came to her desk at Harper & Row as an account of Harriet's comments on her spy route. She recognized the genius of the work and recommended that the writer be worked with to expand and develop what she had submitted. As Ursula Nordstrom notes in her interview with Roni Natov and Geraldine DeLuca for *Lion and the Unicorn,* she took Ms. Zolotow's advice and became Fitzhugh's mentor in the creation of the novel.[8] As Nordstrom notes of Fitzhugh, "she wasn't so sure of herself with *Harriet*" (Natov and DeLuca, 125). But Nordstrom's identification of honesty as the essential feature of Fitzhugh's work and of all great writers and illustrators for children (Natov and DeLuca, 124) is what's crucial in her discussion of her editorial relationship with Fitzhugh, since honesty about one's feelings and desires is what Ole Golly teaches Harriet. Surely, we may suspect that Nordstrom functioned as an Ole Golly for Fitzhugh.

In any case, Ole Golly teaches Harriet to trust and believe in herself. She gives her a healthy ego. Egocentricity, in other words, is not such a bad thing if it reflects a healthy love of self. If innocent, as it always is in a child, it is never simply arrogance, but rather the child's true expression of self, limited as she is in her capacity for empathy by incomplete cognitive development. It is also her only defense against those who would force her to deny her true being. Finally, it is the self-absorption required for self-understanding and for creative expression.

Harriet's Development

The child or artist who never learns what she has in common with all other people, even those whom she perceives as severely flawed, is, however, a crippled creature, and thus Fitzhugh shows us the process whereby Harriet begins to learn to empathize with those who are quite different from her. The central point of Bosmajian's analysis of Fitzhugh's novel is that it unmasks the disconnectedness that characterizes Harriet's (and our) world. Deep and abiding love for that which is outside one's self is, of course, the only means of connection—love of others, love of nature, love of work, love of a supreme being or power or spirit that infuses life with meaning.

Harriet is by far more connected than most of those upon whom she spies. Nevertheless, she feels little connection with those less fortunate than she has been. Her notebook comments are judgments rarely qualified by compassion. She does not understand that people, including her, are always the product of their environments, inhibited and damaged to the extent that they are insufficiently and inappropriately nurtured. She has been lucky enough to have money, comfort, education, and care. She has suffered very little.

It is not until Ole Golly leaves that Harriet learns how dependent she is on others for happiness. Only after she has experienced the pain of isolation and rejection does she begin to understand that love and understanding are essential needs. With Ole Golly gone, Harriet reaches out to her parents and her friends in an attempt to fill the gap. A series of efforts fail. Her parents are hurt when she turns away from their attempts to help her develop her onion part for the Thanksgiving dance. They do not understand her need to write in her notebook and see it as rejection, and she does not understand their reaction. Playing tag, when she does not like the game but needs to avoid an empty house, she forgets about and loses her notebook, which is found and read by her classmates. In response to all the unpleasant comments Harriet wrote about them, her friends then exclude and harass her.

She considers changing, for example, not taking a tomato sandwich for lunch, but Ole Golly has taught her well. Most children would conform to end the alienation that Harriet experiences, but Harriet is too sure and fond of herself to do so. At one point she analyzes her friends' behavior in her notebook, speculating about how Ole Golly would see it: "THEY'RE TRYING TO CONTROL ME AND MAKE ME GIVE UP THIS NOTEBOOK, AND SHE [Ole Golly] ALWAYS SAID THAT PEOPLE WHO TRY TO CONTROL PEOPLE AND CHANGE PEOPLE'S HABITS ARE THE ONES THAT MAKE ALL THE TROUBLE. IF YOU DON'T LIKE SOMEBODY, WALK AWAY, SHE SAID, BUT DON'T TRY AND MAKE THEM LIKE YOU. I THINK SHE WOULD HATE THIS WHOLE THING" (*Harriet*, 226).

Clearly, Harriet here reveals that by writing in her notebook she is trying to control herself—her understanding of the world— and not the world. When her classmates try to control her, rather than conform or retaliate, Harriet turns to what she still has to love—her notebook and writing. She does not try to control other people.

When her mother takes her notebook away, however, Harriet has no safe and trusted outlet for her feelings and thoughts, and she does change. She feels and acts mean, throwing pencils at her classmates, planting a frog in one of their desks, and looking hateful at all of them, even her former friends. Everything that matters to her is gone—Ole Golly, her notebook, her friends, and her schoolwork. Rather than being her allies, her parents side with those who want to control and change Harriet. She is completely alone. Not to fight back at this point would be to surrender her selfhood. Fortunately, even though her parents have never really troubled themselves enough to get to know her, they recognize her aggression as a change in behavior, and they care enough to seek understanding when they need it. They do not attempt, as many parents surely would, merely to reform or discipline Harriet. Had they done so, we must suspect the novel would have ended tragically. Once again, however, Harriet is the fortunate child. If not able or willing to seek understanding on their own, her parents are enlightened and wealthy enough to seek psychiatric help, and Dr. Wagner provides the key to the resolution of Harriet's trouble.

We never know exactly what he tells the Welsches, but what they do afterward allows us to infer what it must have been. They write Ole Golly, who then tells Harriet in a special delivery letter what to do to regain her friends and not deny the truth written in her notebook, how to deal with missing someone who has moved away, and why writing stories is better than taking notes. They visit Harriet's teacher, who then makes Harriet and Beth Ellen coeditors of the class newspaper, and they begin to talk about their lives whenever Harriet is around.

Nothing here criticizes Harriet. What all of these changes strongly imply is rather that her world has failed Harriet. Always it must be remembered that Harriet is 11 years old. She is, furthermore, a young 11 because she has never been required to take much responsibility for others. Ole Golly has cared for her and taught her to care for herself, but no one else has paid much attention. No one else understands Harriet or attempts to explain the world to her. She is, therefore, enormously dependent on Ole Golly, so much so that she cannot deal with her loss or with her friends' rejection alone.

The point is that we are all dependent, which Harriet must learn if she is ever to be able truly to care for herself and others. It is one thing to love oneself and not to fear rejection and harassment—not to let others control one. But it is quite another to live without the love of others—to experience total abandonment. No one can and survive. Babies die. Fear of abandonment leads children to distort who they are and to conform in order to maintain some semblance of connection. Adults, if they continue their deceptions and deny their true feelings, are more dead than alive. Harriet's world is full of such children and adults, and only Ole Golly has stood between her and them. But without Ole Golly, Harriet is lost because she does not know how to get what she needs.

Ole Golly never requires that Harriet understand and love her; indeed, she does not reveal much of herself to Harriet, perhaps because her past causes her great pain. In any case, her relationship with Harriet is much more intellectual than emotional, suggesting that her own need for self-control conflicts with her need for love. Harriet's parents, teachers, and friends are similarly reticent. Thus, Harriet's egocentricity has been allowed mostly to go unchallenged. She has had only to care for herself. She has never been required to see from another's point of view. She has never been required to see how much she, like everyone, needs love, and she must if she is ever to understand and love others—if she is ever to be a writer. Indeed, Harriet has never been required or allowed to do much of anything; she has been rather thoroughly taken care of—by a nurse, a cook, a private school. Thus, she takes and seldom gives.

So she needs Ole Golly's advice that she apologize and lie to her friends. She needs a way to give that does not compromise her and that, nevertheless, respects their feelings. To lie about her notes is the way to regain her friendships. She maintains her sense of the notes as expressions of her honest feelings and thoughts, but she honors her friend's pain upon hearing the notes read aloud to their classmates. She had never intended that anyone read her notebooks. She is not responsible for their pain. She does not really think they should have been hurt. But she can lie and apologize and thereby acknowledge their feelings at no price to her or to them. Harriet also needs Ole Golly's advice that she get busy writing stories, and she needs her job as editor. Writing is another form of giving. At its best, as Ole Golly notes, "writing is to put love into the world, not to use against your friends" (*Harriet,* 278). Finally, Harriet needs her parents. She needs to know what they think and feel and do. She needs them present and interested in her life.

Everyone in Harriet's world, in other words, is isolated—the nonconformist from others and the conformist from her or his true self. Ole Golly provides insight into the only possible way out of this isolation. The only bridge between people is love such as Ole Golly shows her mother, Harriet, and Mr. Waldenstein, such as she describes in her quotation of a passage from Dostoyevsky. The passage advises, "Love all God's creation" (*Harriet,* 22), and promises that "if you love everything, you will perceive the divine mystery of things. Once you perceive it, you will begin to comprehend it better every day. And you will come at last to love the whole world with an all-embracing love" (*Harriet,* 24).

At this early point in the novel, Harriet reveals her selfishness by her misunderstanding of the quotation. Her response is "I want to know everything, everything" (*Harriet*, 24). She fails to hear Ole Golly's caution: "It won't do you a bit of good to know everything if you don't do anything with it" (*Harriet*, 24).

As the story unfolds, so does our awareness of the irony and complexity of the human condition, chiefly as it is reflected in Fitzhugh's characterization of Harriet. She is both the product of her world and its greatest critic, both its victim and its heroine. In other words, Harriet is fully implicated in the world she inhabits, as we all are in our own. Humility is necessary. No one is better than anyone else. One's truth is only one's truth—important, even vital, to one's life, but not unchanging or universal.

By the end of the novel, Harriet has begun to understand human interdependence and to empathize with others. She has tried to be "AN ONION ... A BENCH IN THE PARK, AN OLD SWEATER, A CAT, AND MY MUG IN THE BATHROOM" (*Harriet*, 295). She has "made herself walk in Sport's shoes, feeling the holes in his socks rub against his ankles. She pretended she had an itchy nose when Janie put up one abstracted hand to scratch. She felt what it would feel like to have freckles and yellow hair like Janie, then funny ears and skinny shoulders like Sport" (*Harriet*, 297). She concludes, "OLE GOLLY IS RIGHT. SOMETIMES YOU HAVE TO LIE" (297). She and her friends are back together, each accepting the other for who she or he is. Janie and Sport wait in silence until she finishes writing in her notebook. Then "all three of them turned and walked along the river" (298).

Given her environment, Harriet has come a long way. Certainly, her last response to Marion Hawthorne and the three other girls playing bridge suggests that Harriet has acquired at least some empathy even for those whom she does not admire: "I'm glad my life is different. I bet they'll be doing that the rest of their lives—and she felt rather sorry for them for a moment. But only for a moment. As she walked along the street, she thought, I have a nice life. With or without Ole Golly, I have a nice life" (*Harriet*, 293). I have even argued (Wolf, 125) that Harriet has begun to learn the meaning of the Dostoyevsky passage, as proven by her restatement of it in her own words: "SOME PEOPLE ARE ONE

WAY AND SOME PEOPLE ARE ANOTHER AND THAT'S THAT" (*Harriet,* 277).

Harriet is no saint; she does not at the end "love the whole world with an all-embracing love." Human beings rarely—if ever—get to that state. But Harriet has begun to see "the divine mystery in things" (*Harriet,* 24). She sees "THAT'S THAT." She has a glimmer of the wisdom that informs Fitzhugh's novel.

Themes

Harriet the Spy shows us that to be human is to be both uniquely oneself and the product of an environment. It is to love oneself and others in accordance with one's needs and circumstances at the moment. It is, to use existential terminology, both to be and to become—to perceive and experience the ideal and then by some shift of perception or experience to move on to disorder and confusion, to arrive at another experience of perfect being, and to repeat the whole process over and over again. Moving between being and becoming, between vision and action, between self and others, between independence and dependence, humans strive for perfection and are always imperfect—caught between contradictory needs and impulses and demands. Always in process, always changing, such creatures can never fully understand themselves and can never be fully understood. Each human being is "the divine mystery" incarnate. This is both the glory and the challenge of humanity. We can know, and we can never know. We can see enough to realize how much we don't see. To assert one's intellect in the face of such mystery is only to deny reality. The only meaningful posture is humility and compassion—or love.

This is the wisdom that Harriet begins to learn. Bosmajian points to how *Harriet the Spy* resembles "*King Lear,* where a 'very foolish fond old man' promises his daughter that he and she will sing like birds in the cage 'and take upon's the mystery of things, as if we were God's spies'" (*Bosmajian,* 82). Nodelman is the first to see Harriet as assuming a godlike stance. He notes her posture when she plays town and her interest in the Greek gods as a result of Ole Golly's characterization of them as spies. He is, of course, concerned to establish her arrogance. Bosmajian goes beyond recognizing Harriet's arrogance to explore her glory as one of "god's spies." In her words, "the child takes in the world as if she were God's spy" (*Bosmajian,* 77). Without minimizing Ole Golly's humanness, Bosmajian also explores her mythical role as the wise woman or fairy godmother or god. Especially interesting is her pointing out that "'golly' is the diminutive substitute for God in oaths and exclamations" (*Bosmajian,* 78). Paul enriches Bosmajian's observations by noting that Harriet's writing is essentially gossip, which Patricia Meyer Spacks in *Gossip* exonerates as originally meaning "god-related" (Paul, 71).

God's spy is, of course, an apt metaphor for how we have often thought of children since the time of Wordsworth and the romantics.[9] Innocent, trusting, and uncorrupted, they—we sometimes are able to believe—are in contact with the divine in a way that conscious, frightened, and flawed adults find impossible. Fitzhugh incorporates this use of the metaphor in her characterization of Harriet, but without ignoring the arrogance, cruelty, and selfishness of the egocentric child. The essence of Fitzhugh's presentation of Harriet as a heroine is as God's spy, much like Carroll's of Alice, Twain's of Huckleberry Finn, and Salinger's of Holden Caulfield.[10] All of these children are innocent, vital outsiders eager to figure out what the world is all about. All are better than the world they seek to find a place in—mostly because their hearts are alive and responsive and they are innocent of their own fallibility. We see Harriet's vitality in her fascination with the world, in her bottomless appetite for information about people, in her insatiable curiosity. We see her innocence in her belief that she can know everything. We see that spying is clearly her lifeline in a world characterized by disconnectedness.

Harriet as a Writer

But as long as Harriet spies for herself alone, she runs the risk of mistaking herself for God. Until she confronts her own vulnerability, she lacks empathy, and as long as she fails to feel others' need for love and acceptance, she excludes herself from "the divine mystery." She also has no need to share her understanding of life. She remains a taker (of notes, primarily), an observer, an outsider, a child. Only after her own experience of vulnerability fosters compassion for others, does she truly begin her career as God's spy, beginning to share her gossip with others.

"God's spy" has been a metaphor for the artist as long as it has been for the child.[11] The romantics saw the artist as a unique individual who possesses a stronger connection with the divine (due to an intense sensibility) than the average person and who consequently preserves this connection into adulthood when others may lose it. Certainly, this description of the artist fits Harriet (and Fitzhugh).

But until Harriet understands that "SOME PEOPLE ARE ONE WAY AND SOME PEOPLE ARE ANOTHER AND THAT'S THAT," she has no reason to communicate with others. She does not reach this understanding until she has experienced her own need for and right to acceptance for who she is. Isolated and misunderstood, she at last recognizes others' need for acceptance even when she does not understand and could not stand to be like them. In other words, by nature, she is compelled to investigate how and why people live as they do, but before she is ready to write, she must learn that the reasons for an individual's choices and behavior (including her own), although worthy of attention, exploration, and appreciation, are ultimately beyond her understanding. She must learn to love and to perceive "the divine mystery," for then she "will comprehend it better every day . . . [and] come at last to love the whole world with an all-embracing love" (*Harriet,* 24).

Harriet the Spy, as I have noted throughout, is as much a *Künstlerroman* as a *Bildungsroman.* During the same year that Beebe published his study of the *Künstlerroman* and long before Huf's *Portrait of the Artist as a Young Woman* or any of the other recent feminist studies of the female artist,[12] Fitzhugh gave us this insightful portrait of the artist as a girl. Indeed, this aspect of *Harriet the Spy* is an incredible accomplishment and, therefore, worthy of special attention.

The only critics to focus on Harriet as a budding writer are Francis Molson and Lissa Paul. Molson's main contribution to our understanding of Harriet as a writer is his analysis of the importance of her notebook. He recognizes it as the means whereby she practices writing—not merely as the selection and organization of words, but also as a thinking tool—as a way of organizing and understanding herself, what she observes, and the relationship between the two. He comments on her shuttling between description and analysis and on her growing ability with the latter as she acquires self-understanding. He speaks to the role of the imagination in her acquiring that understanding. He also sees that "spying, with its virtually exclusive concern for the quickly observable, was too restrictive, and her imagination suffered. Like a cartoonist, she saw only one or two physical features or actions and forced these to represent the whole person" (Molson, 970). As a spy, Harriet is, therefore, a remarkable tool for Fitzhugh's witty and sharp satire. But, as Molson points out, by increasing her capacity for empathy, Harriet develops her imagination and, I might add, allows Fitzhugh to deepen the novel's significance. What Molson fails to consider is the role of Harriet's egocentricity. Paul focuses sharply on this feature, noting that Harriet "says all the things that all of us want to say but don't dare" (Paul, 72).

Beebe and Huf, like many others (Meyer Abrams, Milton C. Nahm, and Dorothy L. Sayers, for example, cited in note 11) who have studied individual writers or the characteristics of writers in general, emphasize that writers often display what can seem like monstrous egotism, and readers have traditionally been willing to forgive any display of ego (at least in male writers) for the sake of the story. Perhaps it takes abundant self-love to believe one has something worth saying to others. Surely it does to spend the long hours alone, exploring one's own mind. Such a person must be an introvert, and psychologists tell us that one's orientation inward or outward is probably inborn.[13] So the extent of one's self-involvement may very well be genetically determined— or at least indicated and then determined by the influence of environment on this inborn tendency. But self-involvement is not necessarily egotism. Since the time of romantics, there has been a tendency to see artists as godlike (Byronic) as well as the tendency to see them as god's spies (Wordsworthian). Both tendencies require artists to see themselves as special and gifted. Both require pride, but the latter is grounded in humility and service. Fitzhugh's view is the latter. What's more, she rejects the former as a real possibility. She shows that the more thoroughgoing the egocentricity, the less likely any writing will be done, for the writer feels no need to reach out to others.

But if Fitzhugh shows that Harriet needs to move beyond self-love to love of others, she does not condemn her for her egocentricity, nor does she in any way criticize genuine self-love. Quite to the contrary, she celebrates Harriet's love of self as essential to her worth as a person, to her capacity to love others, and to her ever becoming a writer. Harriet is not perfect. Fitzhugh and Harriet are well aware of Harriet's flaws, most of which result from her abundant energy. But she loves herself. She loves her mind, her gift for words, the pursuit of information and understanding, and the joy of communication. She loves her life, and she is proud to be different—to be a loner and an eccentric. Surely, she was born to become much of who she now is. She would not, however, be as content with herself as she is from the beginning of the book had it not been for her fortunate circumstances, especially Ole Golly, who has given her unconditional love, that is, permission to be herself.

That Fitzhugh recognized the need for a woman as role model and mother in the life of a girl born to be an artist is remarkable. Given her own absent mother and her lifelong grief over her absence, perhaps she created what she knew she had missed and always needed. In any case, her insight and creation is amazing in light of the usual absence of strong, nurturing adult women in *Künstlerromane* by women. Huf points out that female artists generally portray themselves as self-created, lamenting the absence of role models (Huf, 153–55). What's more, the largest obstacle to women's achieving careers as writers is the lack of permission in their environments for them to be what they feel they were born to be. In other words, brought up to think of others first and to develop great powers of empathy, women have been discouraged from loving themselves enough to pursue self-realization. They have been taught to see their desire to write as selfish and egotistical, and they have become writers, therefore, only after enormous internal struggle and at great psychological cost (Huf, 5–12, 150–51). The wonder of *Harriet the Spy,* as Paul points out, is that Harriet "resolves the splits—between life and art, between truth and lying, and between gossip and fiction— that destroy many women writers" (Paul, 72).

There is nothing in *Harriet the Spy* that questions or criticizes Harriet's self-love, even when she is selfish and unsympathetic. The novel is an unqualified celebration of self-love as necessary in a developing writer. Indeed, as I have already discussed, the novel shows that love of others, as psychologists these days are always saying, is firmly rooted in self-love.[14] What must be transcended by a writer (and any child who is to mature) is not self-love or even selfishness, but egocentricity, that is, the inability to see from others' points of view. But the novel does not criticize the child for this inability. It rather seems to accept as a given that to be human is essentially to be egocentric and that to be empathetic is difficult for most of us and impossible when our environment is not supportive, especially when we are cognitively and emotionally unready, as we must be during childhood. Thus, Fitzhugh emphasizes that self-love is essential in a writer's childhood and that empathy, although ultimately necessary to the writer, is secondary in her development.

Another amazing feature of Fitzhugh's novel is Harriet's lack of shame when her friends read the unflattering things that she has written about them. Earlier, when I noted the parallels between Marijane the Spy and Harriet the Spy, I mentioned that they differ in regard to shame. Marijane assumes responsibility for her hurtful treatment of Millicent, even though she had not been intentionally or consciously malicious. She recognizes Millicent's pain and identifies her own behavior as its source. She undergoes a "fortunate fall"—that is, she falls from innocence into consciousness of her capacity to hurt others. Having done so, she experiences intense guilt, or shame, which leads her to accept

responsibility for the effects she has on others and to change herself to prevent any recurrence of such an experience.
Opinions vary about the value of shame. The traditional view,
still that of many contemporary theologians, is that it is the
source of conscience, social responsibility, maturity, and often religious conviction. In other words, it is the means to the fortunate
fall.[15] But the last 25 years have produced many case studies in
which shame emerges as a psychological block that prevents or
at least inhibits individuals' realization of their potential (Bradshaw, 243–45). In light of these contradictory views of shame,
Fitzhugh's portrait of Harriet as refusing to judge writing in her
notebook as wrong is extremely interesting, as is Ole Golly's advice that Harriet must lie about what she wrote to regain her
friendships.
Harriet does not take responsibility for her friends' pain. She
feels no shame. Rather depression and then rage are her very
healthy responses to her classmates' harassment. The only adult
she fully respects does not suggest that she should feel guilty
about what she has done. Yet Harriet matures as a result of the
experience. She takes responsibility for the situation, without
blaming or denying herself, by telling her friends that her comments about them were lies. The experience of isolation teaches
her something about herself, and it is her increased self-knowledge that results in her increased empathy. Made aware of her
own vulnerability, she begins to perceive how vulnerable others
are.
To a large extent, the process Harriet undergoes could be described as normal cognitive development. If developmental psychologists are correct, children are really incapable of altruism
resulting from empathy with those very unlike themselves until
they acquire the ability to do formal operations, which involves a
cognitive shift that may occur around 11 years of age.[16] In other
words, Harriet's experience of rejection comes at a time when she
is ready to learn from it.
The central point is that shame requires some rejection of self,
some sense that one's own desires and truth not only conflict with
those of others, but also cause them pain. It requires judgment

and condemnation of one's acts and can cause great distress for young children and other highly sensitive individuals. It conditions a person to think of others, but it can also result in excessive self-denial, as it has in many women, inhibiting the development of many female artists and surely preventing the development of some. Finally, we must question the value of behavior motivated by shame rather than love, no matter how much we may wish to foster altruism.

In any case, Fitzhugh and Ole Golly do not require Harriet to be shamed, and the novel implies that unqualified self-love is necessary to her development as a writer, as has already been discussed. Also important, however, is the writer's connection with the world. This connection makes self-exploration meaningful, providing the means whereby the writer comes to see herself in others and to see others in herself and to be intrigued by what she does not and perhaps never will understand. In addition, self-love makes the solitude required by writing enjoyable. Loving herself, the writer can be alone and not be lonely, suggesting the resolution of a major conflict in many writer's lives.[17]

But were self-love the entire solution, *Harriet the Spy* would never have been written, and Harriet would not be as preoccupied with Harrison Withers's isolation as she is. Her response to him in Book 1, in fact, sets up a major concern of the novel, that is, the deadening effects of emotional isolation. Book 2 explores its effects on Harriet, and Book 3 indicates the solution—being loved by others. Harriet correctly identifies the greatest obstacle to her becoming a writer—her fear of loneliness.

This fear suggests that she knows unconsciously that she is trapped in her own ego and does not know how to break out, and, indeed, Book 2 reveals that this is the case. First, Ole Golly having left, she confronts her dependence, that is, her need for love and understanding. Second, she shows that she does not know how to take emotional responsibility for herself. She merely expects others to understand and love her, never realizing that she might let them know her ideas and feelings or find out what theirs are. With the help of Dr. Wagner, her parents, Ole Golly, and her teachers, Harriet finally begins to take emotional responsibility for herself. She begins to communicate with others. But first she had to experience her vulnerability, her need for others, her insufficiency. She had to experience the isolation she had instinctively feared when spying on Harrison Withers and to discover the limits of her considerable self-love. Having done so, she is ready to try to explain herself to others and to try to understand and explain others to herself. "SOME PEOPLE ARE ONE WAY AND SOME ARE ANOTHER WAY AND THAT'S THAT" (*Harriet*, 277).

Conclusion

Loneliness is the principal emotional illness in Harriet's world, and quite obviously love is its antidote. In a fairy tale, people come to love each other and live happily ever after, as would we all if love were so easy to come by and keep. In the realistic *Harriet the Spy*, we see why it is not. We see the necessity for self-love and the obstacles to it. We see the essential vulnerability of every individual and the fear it engenders, especially in children, who must depend on others for the satisfaction of their needs for love and understanding. We see that even those who truly love themselves must communicate to bridge the gap between themselves and others, but that egocentricity often prevents or inhibits communication. Finally, we see that only those who love themselves and accept their essential dependence will attempt communication.

But what Harriet learns does not assure that she will live happily ever after—far from it. She has changed so little that Perry Nodelman could say that she "does not change" (Nodelman, 136). By the end of the novel, she has confronted her need for others, she has demonstrated empathy, and she has exhibited some humility. Her situation has changed, and in response, so has she— but only a little. I don't mean to minimize the shift in cognition she experiences and, thereby, to contradict what I have said about it throughout this chapter. Learning to see from others' points of view is a major step in human development. But it is not accomplished over night. As Harriet's newspaper stories reveal, although she is often empathetic, she continues to judge people harshly: "MRS. AGATHA K. PLUMBER IS . . . A VERY STUPID LADY" (*Harriet*, 284) and "FRANCA DEI SANTI HAS ONE OF THE DUMBEST FACES YOU COULD EVER HOPE TO SEE" (*Harriet*, 285). That she does so for others' consideration not only indicates her willingness to reach out for their understanding and appreciation, it also makes her vulnerable, as Harriet realizes all too well. Her horror and joy as she reads her own words reveal her awareness that she risks rejection. Fortunately, only those whom she does not respect (Marion Hawthorne and Rachel Hennessey) express disapproval. But we know that if she ever becomes a published writer, her blunt honesty will meet with great opposition. We need only remember the critical reception of *Harriet the Spy*.

The point is that no matter how much Harriet has changed, the human condition is what it is. As the novel closes, her friends, parents, and teachers understand her a bit better than they had. For the moment, life is not only better, but also joyful. Harriet can be herself and also be loved. But this momentary balance will not last, even though, with luck, Harriet will repeatedly experience it in her life. The conflict between self-love and her need for others will arise again and again as she ages and changes. Like everyone, she remains essentially confined to her ego and yet dependent on others.

She like everyone, will get caught up in her life, understanding of the other may prove impossible, and she will experience rejection. Eventually, she may achieve understanding, communication may mend the breach, and she may reestablish connection. But understanding of others requires similar experience, self-understanding, and emotional distance. It requires great intelligence, sensitivity, and self-love. It is, therefore, often impossible.

Communication is equally difficult, requiring not only love for and understanding of oneself and others but also an inclination for and skill with some medium—words, paint, or music, for example. Fitzhugh suggests that the artist is driven not only to understand life, but also to express that understanding in a certain medium. She further suggests that the decision to share arises from a desire for understanding from others, and that the achievement of understanding depends, in part, on the other half of communication: the audience. She shows that the audience's willingness to receive the artist's expression depends on their possession of many of the same qualities characteristic of the artist. We need only to remember Harriet's bluntness and the people who inhabit her world to understand that her future suffering is inevitable. She has much to learn about successful communication, given this audience. Indeed, many of the people of Harriet's world are so controlled by fear that it is not at all likely that they will ever understand her. They conform to avoid the risk of rejection. A thoroughgoing eccentric at 11 years of age, she risks rejection nearly every time she puts pen to paper. To be sure, her comments about her classmates in the newspaper are much softer than those in her notebook. She has learned. But softness and sympathy are not her gifts. Vitality, curiosity, honesty, and self-love are. Like Fitzhugh, she will, therefore, continue to offend and threaten readers.

Finally, we cannot know whether or not she will always be able to regain a satisfying balance between her need to be herself and her need for love. There are too many unknowns, and the book remains open-ended. What we can know is that she has enormous potential as a writer. As an outsider who loves herself, she has a great deal to say to society about the importance of being oneself and about the dangers of conformity and of other responses to fear of rejection, but only if she learns how to write out of love for her readers and they do not respond with painful and abundant rejection. Truly, Harriet represents both the wonder and the danger of self-love.

Beth Ellen in characteristic repose. Reprinted by permission of Harper & Row and Victor Gollancz, Ltd., from p. 90 of *The Long Secret.* ©1965 by Louise Fitzhugh.

4

Portrait of the Artist as a Girl: *The Long Secret*

When I first read *The Long Secret* in the late sixties, I was disappointed and confused. Like its reviewers, I did not care much for Beth Ellen, I was not very excited by the mystery of who was writing notes that castigated various members of the community of Water Mill, New York, where Beth Ellen's grandmother and Harriet's parents both have summer homes, and I could not see what held the plot together. Its use of two points of view seemed to me a failure, and I was troubled that the Harriet who had mostly delighted me in *Harriet the Spy* here often seemed like someone I wanted to shake. The satire seemed more of Harriet than of those she observed, and the psychological realism seemed much less evident than in *Harriet the Spy,* despite the introduction of the previously taboo subject of menstruation. Finally, I found the setting less stimulating than Harriet's section of New York City. The East Side of New York City is a truly unusual setting in the world of children's books. Stories set in summer homes in areas like southeastern Long Island are not.

The Critics

The Long Secret, often called a sequel to *Harriet the Spy,* has received very little critical attention. Reviewers responded much as

I did, and perhaps its reviews account for the book's subsequent critical neglect, although bad reviews did not ultimately affect *Harriet the Spy*'s reputation. *The Long Secret* has been read and continues to be read by many children, but seldom has it been appreciated or understood in print. Two exceptions to this statement are a review in *Library Journal*[1] and Perry Nodelman's analysis.

Most of its reviewers are as troubled by Fitzhugh's psychological realism as are the reviewers of *Harriet the Spy*. Now ready to recognize that children do enjoy reading about Harriet, reviewers in the *New Yorker*, the *New Statesman, Book Week*, and the *New York Times Book Review*,[2] nevertheless, hint or assert that this novel is more appropriate for adults than children.

Many of them, in any case, do not like *The Long Secret* as well as they like *Harriet the Spy*. For example, according to the *New York Times Book Review*, "it's not as good as 'Harriet the Spy,' because second books never are" (56). There is also the opinion of both the *New Yorker* (219) and *Saturday Review*[3] that Beth Ellen Hansen is not as interesting a character as Harriet.

These opinions suggest how much confusion there is in the reviews over what the book is about. Most see it as a sequel and expect more about Harriet than the book provides or simply see her as the book's heroine, as does the author of the review in the *Times Literary Supplement*.[4] Several reviewers are puzzled by Harriet's seeming as jarring and irritating as she does in this second book and by Fitzhugh's failure to portray her as softened by her experiences in *Harriet the Spy*. In addition to character, plot is variously perceived and misunderstood. The reviewer in *Best Sellers* believes the novel "fast moving and with an atmosphere of suspense,"[5] but *Saturday Review* (45) and the *New York Times Book Review* (56) fault the book's plot as weak, drawn out, and poorly planned.

Only the review in *Library Journal* recognizes Beth Ellen as a major character in the novel and as Harriet's foil, pointing out that they each have something to learn from and to teach the other (5513). This review thus suggests the thematic concerns structuring the novel and opines that "its impact may be more durable than *Harriet the Spy*." Wrong about the book's impact, this reviewer, nonetheless, anticipates the critical defense that Nodelman develops in 1986.

Nodelman understands that Harriet seems startlingly different in *The Long Secret* because we most often see her from Beth Ellen's point of view. He recognizes that the book "seems shapeless," pointing out that "it includes bitter criticism of the sterile inhumanity of international cafe society, the low comedy of the despicably southern Jenkins getting rich quick by making 'toe medicine' out of watermelons, a controversial technical discussion of menstruation, the highly charged melodrama of Beth Ellen's blatantly cruel parents. Fitzhugh gets away with including so many different kinds of characters by focusing on the different ways Harriet and Beth Ellen see them; she alternates between telling the story as Beth Ellen sees it and as Harriet sees it, so that comparisons are inevitable" (Nodelman, 138).

He then proceeds to examine the differences between Harriet and Beth Ellen and to suggest some of the novel's implications. Harriet, like Beth Ellen's mother, is definite; Beth Ellen, indefinite. Harriet is brash; Beth Ellen, shy. The two girls are very nearly opposite. The focus here, however, is on Beth Ellen's anger at her mother for abandoning her and for making her feel unlovable, a secret that she hides under her shyness, just as she conceals her identity as the note writer who perceptively reveals the essential flaws of most of the book's characters. The plot of the novel details the experience whereby she reveals her secret and accepts her true self. In Nodelman's words. "she arrives at the same balanced place Harriet reached, but from an opposite direction; Beth Ellen learns self-love, and Harriet charity" (Nodelman, 139).

A Sequel

In other words, *The Long Secret* is a kind of sequel to *Harriet the Spy*. In various ways, the second novel is like the underside of the first one, more thoroughly drawing from psychological realism and less significantly, satire than the first one. *The Long Secret* is a further exploration of Harriet and of "the wonder and danger of self-love." More directly than does Fitzhugh's first novel, it shows the danger of self-love, here evident in Beth Ellen's and the other characters' difficulties with Harriet and in Harriet's failures to understand others because she judges them in terms of who she is. Nevertheless, the novel is as strong as—perhaps stronger than—*Harriet the Spy* in communicating the wonder of self-love, for in the end, self-love is Beth Ellen's salvation. This second novel is also a further exploration of the source of and the necessity for humility and charity. It is a further lesson for Harriet, who is mistaken in her attempt to solve the mystery of who's writing the notes until the end of the novel. It is also a lesson for Beth Ellen, whose judgments of others in the notes (which eventually she gives up writing) must remind us of the insensitive and yet apt judgments Harriet makes in her notebook. Finally, this novel is a further exploration of the development of the young girl as an artist and is as interesting as *Harriet the Spy* for what it reveals about who Louise Fitzhugh was as a child.

Louise Fitzhugh understood why one must be humble and charitable. She felt herself misunderstood and unloved as a child. She knew firsthand what it felt like to live as a frightened child and to carry that fear into adulthood. She knew how one's childhood shapes one's personality. She knew that self-love evolves out of important adults' unconditional love for one. She lived through a childhood more similar in many ways to Beth Ellen's than to Harriet's—feeling abandoned by her mother, desiring closeness with her paternal grandmother, found wanting by her father, and misunderstood by her stepmother. Her family was very rich and maintained appearances for the outside world, and Louise outwardly conformed completely to their expectations of her, but carried away memories of a childhood full of emotional and physical abuse.

Beth Ellen's Development

If Harriet is Louise Fitzhugh, then, so is Beth Ellen. She is her alter ego, the side of her that allowed her to understand the pain of not being understood and of, therefore, not being adequately loved, the side of her that taught her to love her other side—her intense, energetic, intelligent, perceptive, judgmental, creative self—despite her many flaws. But Beth Ellen also represents the frightened child who must learn to love herself as she is—quite Harriet's opposite.

It is without a doubt Fitzhugh's characterization of Beth Ellen that has stood in the way of critical understanding and appreciation of this novel. Just as the key to her first novel is understanding Harriet, so the key to the second is understanding Beth Ellen. However, Beth Ellen is even more difficult to understand and appreciate than Harriet, for she is, by her very nature, a less interesting and more flawed person than Harriet. Frightened, depressed, repressed, and insecure, Beth Ellen may very well seem without personality. The novel demands more careful and mature readers, therefore, than does *Harriet the Spy*. The mystery of who's writing the notes, as well as Harriet's presence and antics in the novel, works to offset the boredom potential in Beth Ellen's personality. So does the melodrama of the Jenkins family and of the international crowd, including Beth Ellen's mother. But Fitzhugh obviously ran a big risk in allowing Beth Ellen's viewpoint to control as often as it does. During a first reading, many have rejected the book and never returned to it. This is a shame, though, because Perry Nodelman is correct: "*The Long Secret* is . . . as good in its own way as *Harriet the Spy*" (Nodelman, 139).

The characterization of Beth Ellen Hansen is every bit the literary triumph that Harriet M. Welsch represents. Like Harriet, Beth Ellen is fully and perceptively characterized, and she is also one of a kind—as passive as Harriet is active, as quiet as Harriet is loud, as indecisive as Harriet is decisive, as frightened as Harriet is fearless, as insecure about herself as Harriet is sure about herself, as unloved by her parents as Harriet is loved by hers. In large measure, Fitzhugh characterizes Beth Ellen by juxtaposing the two girls and thereby revealing the contrasts in their feelings and behavior and relationships. Harriet serves to provoke responses from Beth Ellen and to stimulate our awareness and understanding of her. These results would never have been achieved had Harriet been absent. Indeed, had Harriet not criticized Beth

Ellen's lack of ambition, demonstrated the excitement of involvement, and dragged Beth Ellen around in pursuit of the note writer, neither girl would have grown as much as they each have by the end of the novel. At the beginning of the book, Beth Ellen's chief emotion is fear. As Harriet recognizes in *Harriet the Spy,* Beth Ellen appears to be afraid of everything. In *The Long Secret,* we are shown that she fears being yelled at, losing her temper, riding her bike, being caught while spying, drowning while swimming at the beach, crying in front of her grandmother, getting caught up in the rough-and-tumble of the Jenkins family, driving with her stepfather, being alone in a bar, and being deserted by her mother and grandmother. When she is not being afraid, she is numb and tired. She spends much time lying or sitting around listlessly, and several times she has long crying bouts. This combination of fearfulness, lack of energy, and grief, of course, suggests depression resulting from her having repressed her true feelings, which, as the novel gradually demonstrates, is exactly what has happened.

Beth Ellen loves her grandmother, but rather than feel that love, she instead fears that she will displease her grandmother. Mrs. Hansen has taught Beth Ellen to be a lady, which means that she is never to lose her temper. Once we understand how angry Beth Ellen is, we see what a burden Mrs. Hansen's lessons about being a lady have been. But before we can understand and see the anger, we must understand the fear that keeps the anger a secret. For the long secret that Beth Ellen keeps from herself, all the other characters, and the reader is that she is a very angry girl with a nearly overwhelming desire to lash out at others for their failures to love. Her notes are proof, for example, "JESUS HATES YOU" (*Long Secret,* 2) "DESPISE NOT THY MOTHER WHEN SHE IS OLD" (*Long Secret,* 33), and "HOW SHARPER THAN A SERPENT'S TOOTH IS A ROTTEN PARENT" (*Long Secret,* 250). In essence, she represses anger out of fear of abandonment. Having been abandoned by her mother and father, she does not trust her grandmother or anyone else not to do the same. So she hides her true feelings and tries to do what others expect of her, especially her grandmother. She understands that she is to be a lady, a girl who will grow up to be rich, get married, have children, and do nothing. But obviously she is not the person she is expected to be, and trying to be what she is not makes her furious, which in turn keeps her frightened, because at any moment her anger might show, might displease her grandmother or someone else, and might result in her abandonment.

Beth Ellen is a very unhappy girl, but she only gradually gets in touch with her unhappiness as the summer proceeds. Harriet is, as was already noted, essential to the process of her doing so. Noticing that Beth Ellen likes to draw, Harriet early on in the novel decides that she will be an artist when she grows up. Beth Ellen asserts that she won't but, rather, will marry a rich man, have babies, and go to Biarritz. Despite Harriet's screaming that Beth Ellen will be boring, she insists that she doesn't "want to be anything at all" (*Long Secret,* 43). Three days later she tries writing again to see if she wants to be a writer, and what she writes is very revealing:

> Dear Me,
>   Why am I so different? Why am I never happy? Is everybody like this or is it just me? I am truly a mouse. I have no desire at all to be myself.
>   Good-bye,
>   Mouse
>   (*Long Secret,* 46)

Harriet has provoked her to think about herself and to recognize her unhappiness. In addition, without realizing it, she here identifies the source of her unhappiness—out of fear, she is not being herself.

Actually, she does want to be herself, as we all do. This letter represents her first step toward finding out who she is and what she wants to do. Her conversation with Harriet about the letter is the next step, for here she recognizes that the problem is that she cannot decide what she wants to do until she knows what she likes. She, of course, already does know, as do we and Harriet, but Beth Ellen will not yet allow her feelings to rise to consciousness. This becomes especially apparent when her grandmother tells her that her mother is coming. Beth Ellen is aware that she does not feel anything. Finally, she begins to think about the possibility that her mother will take her away, asking herself, "Where do I live" (*Long Secret*, 57), and then she begins to cry. The tears here are as much grief over not knowing what she feels as they are over fear of losing her home with her grandmother. Symbolically, her question is as much about her internal home— her true self—as about her external home. It has to remind us of Harriet's earlier irritated comment that she wonders sometimes where Beth Ellen keeps herself (*Long Secret*, 38).

Zeeney, Beth Ellen's mother, also provokes her to get in touch with who she really is and what she really wants. Zeeney returns to take over Beth Ellen's life and to try to make her into Zeeney's image of what her daughter should be. Suddenly, she is called Beth, her hair is straightened, and she is dressed up every afternoon to spend the rest of the day and evening at some social event that appeals to her mother and that is inappropriate and boring for a child. Her mother both controls and ignores her. Beth Ellen is miserable, but she does not rebel, although she thinks about ducking her head under the water in the bath and ruining her hair. Realizing that that's exactly what Harriet would do, she bursts into laughter, upsetting her mother and getting some relief from the situation.

Self-love
Harriet thus continues to be important as Beth Ellen deals with her mother. She is a role model for Beth Ellen, someone who will always be herself and who will resist all efforts to make her be anything else. Even before her mother arrives, Beth Ellen recognizes that she likes Harriet and identifies the reason: "Hurrying after Harriet made her feel curiously liberated, as though she could be a child and it was all right. Harriet always gave her this feeling. It was one of the few things she really liked about Harriet, as a matter of fact, because the principal feeling she felt when with Harriet was one of being continually jarred" (*Long Secret*, 80). Later Beth Ellen elaborates on Harriet's importance to

her. Riding in the basket of Harriet's bike, "she felt oddly protected. Whatever one thinks of Harriet, she thought to herself, one always feels safe with her. Even her rudeness was better than the icy chill of polite parents. She thought what she had thought the other day, that being with Harriet made her feel that she could be a child for once. She felt happy feeling a child. Most of the time she felt like a troll" (*Long Secret*, 221).

A child is, of course, what Beth Ellen, like Harriet, fundamentally is—self-centered, loud, and full of energy. When she allows herself to be who she is, she is happy. When she tries, as she does most of the time, to be what others want her to be—an adult chiefly—she feels like a troll. The point clearly is to be who you are, as Harriet always is.

But Beth Ellen is not yet ready to accept this truth. Before she does, she has a few more things to learn. First, the Preacher, an old black man who lives off in the woods, must tell the girls about the sharecroppers and migrant workers of his former church, who are tired of waiting for their reward on this earth or in heaven. His story makes Beth Ellen realize that she, too, is tired. She, too, has tried to be good and to rely on God and others to reward her. They have not, and, like the members of the Preacher's church, she is no longer willing to wait and can no longer believe that "the meek shall inherit the earth."

Having realized she is no longer willing to allow others to choose for her, she announces to her mother that she intends to be an artist when she grows up. Appalled, Zeeney insists that she will never have a profession of any kind. She laughs at and chastises her daughter, but rather than being crushed, Beth Ellen is certain that she has chosen wisely and continues to assert herself with Zeeney and her stepfather, Wallace. Her doing so leads her mother to insist that her grandmother has erred in rearing Beth Ellen and that she will, therefore, take her away to correct her grandmother's mistakes. This is the last straw for Beth Ellen, who throws a huge temper tantrum. She can no longer contain her anger and slams doors, floods her bathroom and bedroom, throws things, and screams.

Finally, her grandmother, understanding how she feels, points out that "shy people are angry people" (*Long Secret,* 260) and explains that although "it's important to be a lady, . . . not if you lose everything in the process, not if you lose yourself" (*Long Secret,* 261). She tells Beth Ellen that we always need to know what we feel, even if it's anger, and that sometimes we must express our feelings because otherwise we get into trouble. Only then can Beth Ellen tell her how much she dislikes Zeeney and Wallace and wishes to live with her, only to discover that this, too, is her grandmother's wish. At this point, Beth Ellen has discovered the answer to "where do I live?": "In her head rang over and over the phrase, I live somewhere, I live somewhere, I live somewhere" (*Long Secret,* 262). Remembering that her question symbolized her desire to be her self as well as her need to feel at home in her grandmother's house, we must recognize the double significance of her assertion that she lives somewhere. She has released her anger, and no longer needing to repress it, she is free of fear and free to feel whatever she feels. She is free to be and to love herself. The result is a burst of energy and happiness, expressed in behavior that—significantly—reminds her of Harriet. She yells and runs and laughs and rudely asserts her own opinion, even after Harriet finds the book underlined in red pencil that proves Beth Ellen wrote the notes. She knows she will never "have to anymore" (*Long Secret,* 274), for she no longer has to keep her anger or any of her feelings a secret from herself.

Harriet's Development

The Long Secret is a sequel for two reasons: first, because Beth Ellen's journey is the same one taken by Harriet, but from the opposite direction, and second, because here continues the story of Harriet's slow development of humility and charity. As Harriet is Beth Ellen's teacher on her journey, so Beth Ellen is hers. Beth Ellen is a further lesson for Harriet that we cannot always trust appearances and that we can never understand another human being except to the extent that she is willing and able to tell us who she is. Beth Ellen manages to hide her identity as the writer of the notes until nearly the end of the novel, despite Harriet's constant companionship and her dogged pursuit of the note writer's identity.

Beth Ellen provides, in other words, even more convincing proof than Harriet encountered in the first novel that our connection with (love for) others and the universe depends on our respect for mystery and our awareness of our own fallibility. It is open to question how much Harriet comes to understand of Beth Ellen. For here, she continues to be her essential self. Usually Harriet is blinded by egocentricity, always she is driven by her bottomless appetite for knowledge, and often she is insensitive to others, especially to Beth Ellen. But there is abundant evidence that Harriet has already changed and continues to change as the novel's action unfolds.

The most important difference between Harriet in the first novel and in the second is that here she is much more an insider. She and her parents have a warm and open relationship. She and Beth Ellen build a closer friendship than Harriet has with either Janie or Sport. Harriet works off and on throughout the novel on various stories, striving to develop her craft as a writer. Finally, she spends considerable time and energy with the question of whether or not there is a God. In all of these ways, then, she experiences or works toward strengthened connections with others and the universe.

Harriet's Parents

Perhaps because it is summer, perhaps because of what happens in *Harriet the Spy,* her mother is always at home and always there for Harriet. On the weekends, both parents spend time with her. Her father brings Janie from town to visit one weekend. He prepares a clambake for the Welsches and Beth Ellen and Janie. Harriet's friends sleep over. When Harriet has questions about religion or Beth Ellen's mother, she has serious conversations with both parents, who seem like wise, ideal parents in this book. They try to answer Harriet's questions, but they do not allow her to invade their privacy. They strive for a careful balance between intimacy and distance. They try to give Harriet what she wants, but not without some concern that she learn that she "can't have everything" (*Long Secret,* 202).

The most interesting scene involving Harriet and her mother occurs at the Shark's Tooth Inn, to which Harriet persuades her mother to go so that she can watch what happens between Beth Ellen, Zeeney, Wallace, Agatha Plumber (who, it turns out, owns the restaurant), and Bunny (the piano player on whom Harriet and Beth Ellen have spied all summer, mostly because Beth Ellen has a crush on him). Mrs. Welsch is not quite comfortable with taking a child to a bar, but she is also quite clearly intrigued by the possibility of seeing Zeeney Hansen, whom her husband had dated as an adolescent. Limited to Harriet's point of view, we are not told what her mother is thinking and feeling. But it is evident that more is going on than Harriet understands. Her mother is disturbed by Harriet's inability to conceal her curiosity and tries to restrain her from standing up or speaking out, but she gets as caught up as Harriet in the extravagant behavior of the party they are watching. Fascinated by the interactions among the people at Zeeney's table, pleased by a brief encounter with and triumph over Zeeney, and also worried by what she sees happening to Beth Ellen, Mrs. Welsch decides to stay for dinner, although she had insisted to Harriet that they would not do so. Then, when Zeeney leaves without Beth Ellen, Harriet's mother steps in, takes both girls home, feeds them, and puts them to bed. A person in her own right, with her own life and weaknesses and strengths, Mrs. Welsch is here a much better mother than she is in *Harriet the Spy.*

Harriet's Friendship with Beth Ellen

Mrs. Welsch is also more sensitive to Beth Ellen than is Harriet. Indeed, much of what happens in this book between the two girls concerns their both becoming increasingly aware of Harriet's insensitivity to Beth Ellen. We have looked at Beth Ellen's awareness of Harriet's being jarring and rude and of her acceptance of that side of Harriet as compensated for by the safety of being with someone who is always honest. Beth Ellen also comes to realize that Harriet can't really help herself. Obsessed with finding out about whatever attracts her attention, Harriet is so driven that it seldom occurs to her to notice what her friend might be feeling and thinking. She has her pegged as frightened—a mouse—and she responds to her as such, trying to bully and boss her into what Harriet wants and believes best. Thus, she persuades Beth Ellen to ride her bike to the Jenkins', to spy, to swim, to help out in Harriet's quest to solve the mystery of the notes, to consider being an artist, to let Harriet meet her parents, and to do a great many other things that interest Harriet. She keeps Beth Ellen involved, despite her fear, and in the process, each supplies the other with friendship of a sort.

Just as Beth Ellen's responses to Harriet make us aware of what's wrong with their friendship, so do those of another child, Jessie Mae Jenkins. The eldest daughter of a poor southern family who now live on the other side of Water Mill, Jessie Mae has a considerably stronger ego than does Beth Ellen. Intending to be a preacher, she is Harriet's prime suspect as the note writer because the notes reveal a familiarity with the Bible. She is also considerably more thoughtful of others than is Harriet, except when they are unkind. Thus, she points out to both girls that Harriet does not treat Beth Ellen as a friend should—with kindness and consideration. Both are startled; Harriet is outraged and Beth Ellen, wildly amused. "Beth Ellen began to like Jessie Mae . . . [;] she seemed to be able to say the most devastating things to Harriet, the kind of things that Beth Ellen only thought of later, on her way home, when it was too late" (*Long Secret,* 71). Obviously, Beth Ellen needs to express her feelings for Harriet to her, and Harriet needs to think more about Beth Ellen and less about herself.

In the course of the novel, Beth Ellen learns to stand up for herself with Harriet and to earn her admiration. She refuses to agree that Jessie Mae is the note writer, suggesting that the Preacher is just as likely a candidate. She stops Harriet's calling her "Mouse." She never tells Harriet what Harriet had failed to hear while spying on Beth Ellen and Jessie Mae on the porch at the Shark's Tooth Inn, and she keeps her identity as the note writer secret until the very end.

Equally important, Harriet learns to respect and care for Beth Ellen. The day after Zeeney's arrival, Harriet tries to pump Beth Ellen, who refuses to talk. Eventually, Harriet notices "that Beth Ellen's eyes were red and swollen. She's been crying, she thought. Maybe they're hateful and she isn't telling me" (*Long Secret*, 173). For a few minutes at least, she is then gentler than she was. The night after the fiasco at the Shark's Tooth Inn, Beth can't keep from crying, and Harriet silently holds her hand until she stops. Most important, she learns that the note writer is not a maniac, as she had thought, but rather her troubled friend. She realizes that Beth Ellen is the writer while they are at the Preacher's house. She listens as the Preacher explains that his parishioners rejected the Bible's council to expect rewards for virtue only after death. She picks up on Beth Ellen's distress that the Preacher does not seem content with believing "the meek shall inherit the earth." She recognizes that "THE MICE SHALL INHERIT THE EARTH," which is the note the Preacher received, is an alteration of this Biblical line that Beth Ellen would make. But rather than exposing Beth Ellen, she waits until she finds the book Beth Ellen had taken the quotations from, and then she takes it to keep her from writing any further notes. Her act is unnecessary, we know, but it is meant as protection.

Charity

Harriet does not completely understand why Beth Ellen wrote the notes. As the Preacher says, "It is a mystery, . . . but there are a great many mysteries in this life" (*Long Secret*, 232). Once again, Fitzhugh's point is that Harriet must increase her respect for the essential mystery of a fellow human being. In this novel, Fitzhugh has Beth Ellen, who poses a greater challenge than does either Janie or Sport, confront Harriet. Harriet and her other friends are more like each other than Harriet and Beth Ellen are. To begin with, therefore, she has greater respect for them than for Beth Ellen. But Beth Ellen fools Harriet and thereby illustrates once again what Harriet has such a hard time accepting: Harriet cannot know everything. She can learn and learn and learn, but she will always be dependent on others for understanding of who she and they are. She will only know as much about them as they are willing and able to share. Humility and charity are, therefore, absolutely essential.

In contrast, Beth Ellen tries to practice what Harriet is still trying to learn. But Beth Ellen must learn that true humility and charity never are achieved at the expense of one's selfhood. Self-sacrifice, rather, results in misdirected anger such as her note writing and her lethargy. She, like the Preacher's sharecroppers and migrant workers, cannot deny her feelings and needs, waiting for God or others to take care of her. Unintentionally, she will hurt herself and others, for self-denial produces anger, and repressed anger works secretly against its owner and others and results always in unhappiness.

Religion

Fitzhugh's introduction of religion into this novel is one of its most interesting features. The metaphysical base implicit in her use of the Dostoyevsky quotation in *Harriet the Spy* is here made explicit. To be sure, charity is explored in both books primarily as a feature of each girl's psychological development, rather than in religious terms. But in *The Long Secret,* as Harriet confronts yet another human being who is a mystery, she also for the first time in her life considers religious mystery. Once again, she is advised to respect (love) what she does not and perhaps cannot ever understand.

Jessie Mae Jenkins and the Preacher raise the topic of religion for Harriet. Jessie asks Harriet and Beth Ellen why she doesn't see them in Sunday school. Harriet, who never goes, is shocked to discover that Beth Ellen regularly attends both church and

Sunday school in Manhattan, but only church during the summer. Then Jessie Mae goes on to talk of becoming a preacher and of studying the Bible daily with The Preacher, asserting that everything we need to know is in the Bible. Harriet is nonplussed by this whole conversation. A little while later, Harriet and Beth Ellen encounter the Preacher, who asks if they will "enter the kingdom of heaven" and if Harriet knows "the perils of undue curiosity" (*Long Secret*, 84). To the first question, Harriet answers in the affirmative with great certainty. In response to the second, she explodes in anger. Since a major topic of both novels about Harriet is "the perils of undue curiosity," we must see the Preacher as a messenger of truth and Harriet's response as a sign of some uneasiness with her obsession.

These experiences provoke Harriet to ask her father if he is religious, only to be surprised again. He tells her, "I don't follow any organized religion. That is not to say I am not a religious man. I don't know how I could look at those stars and not be a religious man" (*Long Secret*, 133). He goes on to praise the Bible as a fascinating book, whose poetry has never been equaled and to insist that "we should respect someone's religion whether we share it or not" (*Long Secret*, 135). Harriet does not understand, so he explains that no matter how Harriet might feel about other people's religion, they take it seriously, and their seriousness deserves respect, especially when they have thought about their beliefs. He adds that even when they haven't thought through their beliefs, they should be pitied, not scorned.

Harriet still does not understand what her father says. As her next question about fanatics reveals, what she really wants is a way to discount Jessie Mae and the Preacher. Her father's reply does not clarify matters for her, but it is a key passage in the novel. He says that fanatics "tend to think the end justifies the means, ... and that's just stupid. ... How *can* it? When there never *are* any ends ... everything goes on and on ... so it remains we are all *means.* ... I just don't understand why people don't see that. It's what's causing *all* the trouble today" (*Long Secret*, 135–36). This response should recall Harriet's remembering in *Harriet the Spy* that Ole Golly had said that trying to control others is what causes all the trouble. Here again, this time through Mr. Welsch, Fitzhugh considers people who try to change others, thinking that the end—heaven, goodness, knowledge, or whatever—justifies the means. Jessie Mae rushes around after her twin brother Norman, trying to get him to give up his pursuit of money and return to the church. The Preacher tried to keep his church content with the promise of heaven. Beth Ellen sends people notes that point out their flaws. Harriet invades people's privacy in her obsession with seeing.

But Mr. Welsch's comment goes beyond the issue of control to suggest not only what people should not do, but what they might do. He advocates our appreciating the "means" more than we do, or to put it another way, our respecting ourselves for who we are at the moment and others for who they are, thereby honoring each moment and the process of life rather than always focusing on what might or should be. Put yet another way, we might love rather than judge, and not simply because it is better for us psychologically. The stars, the swan skeleton Janie takes back to Manhattan, every person, and every thing are all part of what Mr. Welsch calls the "means" and of what Mrs. Welsch calls "God's . . . beautiful creatures" (*Long Secret,* 138). Charity here takes on religious connotations.

Harriet understands little of what her father says, as her conversation with Janie and Beth Ellen later that night reveals. Still puzzled and curious, Harriet asks if they believe in God. Janie, the scientist, does not. She thinks people made up God to assuage their fears. As if to prove Janie correct, it is frightened Beth Ellen who, although she isn't sure, thinks she believes in God. She recalls the comfort of a beloved grandfather telling her that God is good. But she cannot or will not tell Harriet what it feels like to believe in God, and Harriet's thoughts are full of questions and doubt.

Doggedly, Harriet turns to her mother. Mrs. Welsch says that she believes in God and feels she needs Him for comfort and support, but she also insists that belief is "a purely personal matter" (*Long Secret,* 167) and that Harriet should think about it because only then will she know what she feels. Harriet is very curious to know what believing in God feels like, but she understands and accepts that her mother will not or cannot tell her. Thinking about whether or not she wants there to be a God, Harriet concludes she's not sure because He might spy on her all the time. Turning to her other concern, about whether or not Jessie Mae and the Preacher are fanatics, Harriet asks if fanatics are crazy people who froth at the mouth. Her mother assures her that they are not, but are rather ordinary people whose obsessions are unrecognizable until one gets to know them well. What she says reinforces what Harriet's father says about people's tendency to forget the means in pursuit of the end and what Fitzhugh implies about people's obsessiveness in most of her work. Many—if not most—of Fitzhugh's characters are, by this definition, fanatics. Obsessions drive them to ignore how their behavior negatively affects others and themselves.

Ironically, Harriet's obsession with seeing everything inhibits her seeing. It leads her to ignore the fact that she is invading others' privacy, although she resents any invasion of her own. At some level, she knows that spying is wrong, but her need to see overwhelms this knowledge, and, not recognizing the limitations of spying as a way of knowing, she cannot conceive of God as anything other than a spy. Just as she misses the significance of Beth Ellen's decisions to begin and end writing the notes, she cannot understand what her mother and father tell her about religion. Her obsession with seeing blinds her. Her love of self makes her arrogant. As Beth Ellen's note to her so aptly points out, "HE THAT IS OF PROUD HEART STIRRETH UP STRIFE BUT HE THAT PUTTETH HIS TRUST IN THE LORD SHALL BE MADE FAT" (*Long Secret,* 129). Harriet would see more quickly and truly if she thought less of herself and more of others. If she trusted the "means" or "THE LORD," she would get what she wants or "BE MADE FAT."

On the other hand, Beth Ellen, whose obsession is hiding, sees clearly. Her notes are always perceptive, as are her thoughts about Harriet. Effacing herself, she focuses her attention entirely on others. She watches everyone carefully and judges the extent to which she should mistrust them. She learns to be a very good child, never disobeying and never expressing anger. She relates to God as she relates to people: she never asserts herself out of fear of abandonment. She simply waits for others and for God to take care of her, afraid that any act by her might result in her being rejected.

The Young Girl as an Artist

Once again Fitzhugh's exploration of the female *Künstlerroman* focuses not on discipline, training, or practice as much as on psychological development. Indeed, what she has to say about this development is much the same as what she says in *Harriet the Spy*. What is different is the emphasis. The first novel stresses the role of self-love in that development; the second novel, the role of fear, suffering, and needless self-sacrifice.

The Long Secret is much more typical of the female *Künstlerroman* than *Harriet the Spy*. As Linda Huf points out, the chief problem facing the heroine of most *Künstlerromane* is her social conditioning to care for others before she cares for herself. Such is Beth Ellen's conditioning, but not Harriet's. In this second novel, Fitzhugh continues to emphasize the importance of self-love by including Harriet as a main character, but she also explores the limitations of the traditional sex role in her portrait of Beth Ellen. At 11, arrogant Harriet is already practicing her craft as a writer; at 12, selfless Beth Ellen, despite obvious and recognized talent as a writer and an artist, is unable even to select an occupation. Even Fitzhugh's choice of names seems to reflect her purposes. So often characters named Beth are the good, little girls of fiction, the most notable example being Beth of *Little Women,* who is so pure that she belongs only in heaven. *Harriet,* on the other hand, has none of the same softness, connotations, or associations.

Fitzhugh's emphasis in *The Long Secret* is on Beth Ellen, but not for the sake of portraying the developing artist struggling with her identity as a female, like most other female *Künstlerromane*. The novel is rather severe criticism of the traditional female sex role carried to an extreme. But the difficulty Beth Ellen experiences deciding to become an artist is insignificant in the total picture of psychological damage Fitzhugh attributes to self-lessness. Clearly, she is more concerned to condemn a child's being taught to deny herself than she is to explore a child's conflict between becoming a good woman or becoming an artist. Once Beth Ellen begins to think of herself first, she easily asserts that she will become an artist.

Indeed, Fitzhugh even shows that female conditioning can be an asset for the artist. Most feminist criticism has, of course, argued for the much needed female point of view. Values traditionally associated with the female—empathy, compassion, and cooperation—are seen as necessary in all spheres of life to offset and correct the emphasis on values traditionally associated with the male—aggression, domination, and competition.[6] Here Beth Ellen's sensitivity to others makes her more perceptive and empathetic than Harriet. Her insecurity and lack of self-esteem make her less quick to judge and condemn others than Harriet is, more willing to understand and forgive. Even her notes, in which her buried anger and judgments emerge, frequently offer advice as well as criticism. For example, she tells Harriet not only about the effects of her pride, but also about how to overcome it and to live the good life. It amazes me that Fitzhugh saw much before many feminists (*The Long Secret* was published in 1965) that sensible criticism of traditional sex roles would not condemn one or the other, but would point out the strengths and weaknesses of both and assert the need for balance.

What Fitzhugh says about the development of the young girl as an artist in this second novel is finally what she had already said in *Harriet the Spy*: Art is possible only when the artist is able to balance self-love and charity. Love of work, of others, of life, and of God are rooted in self-love. Love supplies the motivation for creating, but self-love allows the artist to tolerate isolation and provides the content for the art. It is essential. But so is the ability to step out of one's self and to perceive one's self and others truly. Fear often supplies the motivation for doing so, and one's own suffering is often the source of empathy for the pain and peculiarities of others. Charity is as necessary as self-love to a budding female artist. But charity should not require self-sacrifice, nor should self-love allow one to ignore or hurt others. The key is balance such as Harriet achieves at the end of *Harriet the Spy* and Beth Ellen at the end of *The Long Secret*. Neither is, of course, in equilibrium. Harriet gains the capacity for some charity in the first novel, but as the sequel reveals, she is in need of much more, even at the end. Beth Ellen, similarly, acquires some love of self by the end of the novel, but we must suspect that she has only begun to recognize and pursue her need for self-love. They provide an intriguing contrast. Certainly, Beth Ellen is more likeable, especially by the end of the novel, if less interesting and entertaining than Harriet. Surely, she will be more loved than Harriet, but just as surely, Harriet will get more of what she wants than Beth Ellen. And as an artist, Harriet is more likely to succeed than Beth Ellen, even though Beth Ellen is more likely to see and to portray life in depth than is Harriet. But neither is a whole person.

Conclusion

The implications in these two novels for understanding Louise Fitzhugh and her art are fascinating. The details of her life support our seeing her as both Harriet and Beth Ellen and our understanding why, therefore, she was able both to celebrate and to criticize each heroine. But whatever the benefits for her writing, the separation of the self into two characters suggests schizophrenia and serious psychological problems. In some way, the psyche must find a middle ground where the parts of the self may mesh and become one. Fitzhugh portrayed two young female artists who together are a whole person. She never created one character whose personality revealed a completely successful resolution of the conflicts embodied in the contrast between Harriet and Beth Ellen. Her failure to do so suggests that she never managed to resolve her own inner division.

To be fair, many of us are Harriets and many of us are Beth Ellens and very few of us are a perfect balance of the two. Very few of us are even what Fitzhugh was. Whatever the psychological cost of her internal conflict, the artistic achievement represented by *Harriet the Spy* and *The Long Secret* suggests that the conflict was at the heart of her creative genius.

5

Harriet's Mistakes as an Artist: *Nobody's Family Is Going to Change*

Nine years elapsed between the publication of *The Long Secret* and that of *Nobody's Family Is Going to Change*. Fitzhugh's third novel appeared in 1974, a few days after her death. It is about the unhappy Sheridans, an affluent black family who live at Seventy-ninth and East End, not far from where Harriet lives. William Sheridan is assistant district attorney. Virginia (Ginny) Sheridan is his wife, social companion, and the mother of his children, 11-year-old Emancipation (Emma), who wants to be a lawyer (like Fitzhugh's father), and 7-year-old William, Jr. (Willie), who wants to be a tap dancer (like Fitzhugh's mother). Both parents lead a very active social life, so the children are often cared for by their white maid. Conflict arises because their parents want Willie to be a lawyer and Emma to be the wife of a lawyer with two lovely children.

Like *The Long Secret, Nobody's Family Is Going to Change* is narrated by two characters, Emma and Willie. Willie is strongly reminiscent of Harriet. He knows what he wants to be when he grows up, and he is very energetic and positive about life. But like Beth Ellen, he is emotional, rather than intellectual. Emma is also an interesting combination of parts of Harriet and Beth

Ellen. Like Harriet, Emma is an outsider who really doesn't care for many other people. She is also a nontraditional female—overweight, assertive, very intelligent, dressed in jeans and a sweatshirt, and already decided about her future occupation. Like Beth Ellen, she does not love herself, and she is very angry at those who fail to love others—mostly her parents. She does not, however, hide her feelings.

What is interesting in the creation of Emma Sheridan is the open focus on anger. Unlike Harriet and Beth Ellen, she has no wise woman to advise and love her, and she really doesn't like herself. All she has are her considerable intellect, her interest in law, and her common bond with her brother Willie. He does have someone, their Uncle Dipsey Bates, who is a professional dancer. Emma, recognizing the similarities between their situations, is the first in the family to offer Willie support. When pushed hard, their weak mother also comes to his aid. Like Emma, Willie is nontraditional—a sensitive male who wants to be a dancer—and, like Emma, he is misunderstood by and at odds with their parents. Emma is more outspoken in her war with her parents than Willie is, but he is the first to resist actively. She thinks and talks; he acts. Then, too, he loves himself much more than she. For the third time, Fitzhugh writes a novel whose impetus is her need to assert that survival and happiness depend on self-love. But here Emma's viewpoint and anger prevail, and there is no effort comparable to that in Fitzhugh's first two novels to show that charity is also necessary. In this novel, like Harriet, Fitzhugh most often offers judgment, not compassion.

The result is a complex satire, often sharp and hard in tone, that lacks the sensitivity and resonance of Fitzhugh's first two novels. This novel does not achieve the depth of psychological realism now recognized as a principal merit of *Harriet the Spy* and *The Long Secret*. It has, rather, the tone of Harriet's notebook entries. Often outrageously funny, it offers clear-cut judgments of others and very little compassion for anyone but the viewpoint characters. Intellectually, *Nobody's Family Is Going to Change* is a powerhouse, but emotionally, it is very unsatisfying. The anger that drives the book is never resolved or transcended. Willie, although still a small child, gets his chance on Broadway because his mother does eventually side with him against his father. But Emma's viewpoint dominates the novel, and her parents do not change their opinion of her. She does succeed in turning her anger away from herself and toward them. She moves toward self-love. But the novel allows her to conclude that "nobody's family is going to change" and to remain furious with her parents.

In Emma Sheridan, Fitzhugh again explores the inner conflict central in her first two novels, but Emma's situation is much more potentially tragic than either Harriet's or Beth Ellen's. Emma is fat and black. Like Harriet and Beth Ellen, she is gifted and has wealthy parents. But both Harriet and Beth Ellen are loved. Beth Ellen is less sure of her grandmother than Harriet is of Ole Golly, and she has to deal with a mother who has abandoned her. Emma, however, is sure that her parents do not love her. They want her to be what she is not. They are unhappy with her, and she internalizes their unhappiness. In order to save herself, she distances herself from them, perceiving them as the enemy. She feels she cannot afford compassion for them because it would trap her in one way or another and concludes that she must not care what they want. But in doing so, she seems also to conclude that she cannot care about them. Tragically, such may be the case when one is 11. It is, of course, possible for us to care for someone who is not able to value us truly, but only when we are not dependent on them for emotional support.

Nobody's Family Is Going to Change does not offer us this insight, nor does it offer us sufficient understanding of Emma's parents. We may also question whether Emma would ever arrive at the understanding she eventually achieves. *Nobody's Family Is Going to Change* is consequently less successful than either *Harriet the Spy* or *The Long Secret*. It attempts a great deal. It has tremendous energy and intellectual complexity, but it lacks heart. It reflects the kinds of mistakes that we would expect of Harriet as an artist.

The Critics

By and large, those who have written about *Nobody's Family Is Going to Change* have generally offered very similar opinions.

Some reviewers have been more critical than others, but all have agreed that the novel is a work of great power. A major criticism has been that it attempts too much. The reviewer in *Psychology Today* lists "women's liberation, children's rights, and male liberation . . . , with glancing passes at homosexuality, the psychological mechanism behind obesity, and black problems."[1] Alcoholism, battered children, disabilities, and poverty could be added to the list. This review concludes "it's too much for one novel to bear, and Fitzhugh trails off into didacticism" (108). The review in *Publishers Weekly,* which Fitzhugh read and found so devastating the weekend before she died, makes the same criticism, also complaining that problems such as these are too often dealt with in children's literature.[2] Everyone agrees that the novel takes on too many social problems. As Nodelman puts it in his piece for *The Dictionary of Literary Biography,* "Fitzhugh's earlier insistence on respect for individuality here becomes a general attack on discrimination of all sorts" (Nodelman, 140).

A more frequent criticism has been that the book relies on stereotypes or lacks realism. Reviewers for the *Bulletin for the Center for Children's Books, Booklist,* the *New York Times Book Review,* and *Horn Book* all make this criticism.[3] Nodelman concludes that "its characters are deliberately stereotyped, deliberately contrasted with each other, in order to make points" (Nodelman, 140). His emphasis on the book's being heavily involved with its thesis recalls the charge of didacticism leveled in the *Psychology Today* review. Unlike some of the book's reviewers, however, Nodelman understands that its didacticism and use of stereotypes are not necessarily flaws, but rather typical of much satire.

The claim that Fitzhugh fails to provide realism in this novel is, however, countered by many reviewers who see it as brutally honest and realistic, for example, those for the *Times Literary Supplement, Language Arts, Booklist, Childhood Education,* and the *Journal of Reading.*[4] To some extent, we may see this contradiction in the reviews as the result of different understandings of the term *realism.* Some of these reviewers obviously call the book realistic because it deals with unpleasant and controversial realities, rather than offering children a safe, sweet story. But others, such as Sarah Hayes in the *Times Literary Supplement,* are responding to the genius with which Fitzhugh captures Emma's voice and feelings as well as to the complexity with which she conveys young people's egocentricity and the psychodynamics of human relationships. Certainly, for these reasons, although I noted that *Harriet the Spy's* realism had greater depth I credited *Nobody's Family Is Going to Change* with realism when I reviewed it for *Children's Literature.*[5]

Oddly, the reviews of *Nobody's Family Is Going to Change* are more positive than those of *The Long Secret* and *Harriet the Spy,* but they reveal the same confusion about what Fitzhugh was doing and, therefore, offer differing opinions about this novel's merit.

Satire

Thanks to Nodelman, we can now appreciate Fitzhugh as a satirist and praise her strong moral convictions as well as her perceptiveness about human failings. We can credit her near-genius ability to make us laugh at the absurdity of human behavior and recognize the careful patterning and plotting and sense of timing that both create the humor and reveal the complex intellect behind the book. All of Fitzhugh's writing must be evaluated in terms of its uses of satiric techniques if it is to be correctly assessed, but this is especially true of *Nobody's Family Is Going to Change,* for it is the most thoroughly satiric work she wrote. The more satiric a work, the more intellectual and emotionally distanced it will be, which, as I have already indicated, are two important traits of Fitzhugh's last novel.

But we must not forget that Nodelman sees Fitzhugh's satire as thin when she fails to individualize her characters (Nodelman, 13) and that Bosmajian contends that at her best Fitzhugh offers a blend of satire and psychological realism, as she does in *Harriet the Spy* (Bosmajian, 73). In *The Long Secret,* the latter dominates, although satire is certainly evident. In *Nobody's Family Is Going to Change,* the balance swings in the other direction, although most who have written about the novel have seen—if seldom thoroughly understood—only its attention to psychological realism.

Psychological Realism

Child abuse, racism, and homosexuality are not necessarily more realistic than loved children, racial harmony, and the absence of references to sexual behavior in a children's novel. Obviously, any one novel may not deal with some aspect of reality, and just as obviously, a novel that deals with subjects generally not dealt with in children's literature is not necessarily any more realistic than one more conventional in its subject matter. It may be unfortunate that most children's literature did not before the 1960s deal with unpleasant or controversial realities. But any one book cannot be condemned or praised as realistic because it did not or did introduce a topic previously unmentioned in children's books. It could be condemned for its lack of originality or praised for its innovation, but the choice of subject matter does not have anything to do with whether or not the book is realistic. These distinctions have been too seldom understood by reviewers and critics of children's literature.

It is not choice but rather treatment of subject matter that determines a book's realism. That the people, places, and behavior portrayed might exist in reality as it has been or is known is important. So are adequate fullness and complexity in the development of character, setting, and action.

Fitzhugh usually convinces her readers that her settings are real places, although she generally pays less attention to them than to character. Her choice of characters often upsets readers' sense of the way people are. Harriet, Beth Ellen, Emma, and Willie are all atypical children, and adults have often condemned them as unbelievable. Like her protagonists, Fitzhugh's other characters are usually unconventional, if not bizarre. They, furthermore, are usually types. For both reasons, they have repeatedly been dismissed as unrealistic.

But major characters are almost always the only fully developed characters, and the test of realism for any character is not familiarity or full and complex development. We must be able to believe that the character might exist, and the writer must provide us with sufficient understanding of who a character is and of why he or she possesses this personality. But realism is always finally a matter of narrative technique and of fidelity to psychology.

Beginning, it is usually agreed, with Heisenberg's Principle of Uncertainty, the twentieth century has taught us how much what we know is a function of individual perception. As Wayne Booth points out in *The Rhetoric of Fiction,* fiction beginning with James has reflected this lesson in its attention to narrative technique, that is, to capturing one or more characters' points of view, to using one to qualify another, to creating action to undermine or support viewpoints, and to distancing us from the author.[6] The effect is to make the characters seem responsible for our view of reality and to make the test of realism, not merely a matter of probability, but also of the success with which the author captures the narration of one or more characters. This success is, of course, largely dependent on the author's understanding of psychology— thus the term, *psychological realism.*

Narrative Technique

We have already explored the misunderstanding of *Harriet the Spy* and of *The Long Secret* because reviewers and critics have failed to appreciate the skill with which Fitzhugh presents Harriet's and Beth Ellen's points of view. It should not surprise us that there has been similar misunderstanding of *Nobody's Family Is Going to Change.* Willie and Emma have been rejected as unbelievable characters because the reader failed to consider how thoroughly their viewpoints control the novel. Similarly, objections that the parents are not well enough understood reflect the same failure.

Willie's dedication to dancing at the age of seven has resulted in his being seen as unbelievable. Certainly, it is unusual. As the novel itself points out, seven-year-olds change their minds frequently about what they want to be when they grow up. They often have no real idea of what they might be and mix rabbit and superman in with fire fighter and doctor as possibilities. But this is not to say that no seven-year-old knows. There are obvious exceptions, such as Mozart. In geniuses whose talent is present from a very young age, the choice of an occupation may be made very early. Willie is a very gifted dancer, who has been dancing for several years. It is believable that he would know that dancing is and always will be the most important thing in his life. Any child of his age who could get a job dancing on Broadway solely on the basis of performance would have to be exceptional. Such a child might very well feel and be devastated by parents who do not understand his drive and need to dance. Fitzhugh's characterization of Willie by means of his viewpoint is entirely believable if we remember that Willie, like Harriet and Beth Ellen, is atypical.

In any case, although what happens in this novel mainly concerns Willie, Emma's point of view largely controls what we see of and understand about Willie's plight. She, too, is atypical, but her talent is intellectual rather than creative. In this, she is both very similar to and very different from Harriet. Both of them are extremely perceptive, analytical, and judgmental, but Emma lacks Harriet's joy in seeing, understanding, and communicating. In this book, Fitzhugh gives the artist's joy in creating to Willie. To Emma, she gives unhappy insight and judgment. The result is an amazingly sophisticated and bitter analysis of a severely damaged child.

Emma's Personality

Unappreciated for who she is, Emma spends her happiest moments eating and fantasizing. These are, of course, the ways she compensates for her feelings of being unloved and unlovable. In the long run, though, they are more punishing than rewarding or nourishing. Eating makes her increasingly overweight and repulsed by her appearance, and fantasizing results in her being embarrassed because she loses track of reality, is caught by others lost in fantasy, and allows the fantasy to intrude into reality before she realizes what has happened. Furthermore, many of her fantasies of herself as a lawyer in front of the court, usually with her father as district attorney, end in her humiliation because she is perceived as bizarre or incompetent. Her obsessions with food and fantasy, in other words, reflect her self-hatred and self-punishment.

But to say she hates and punishes herself is only to begin to understand who Emma is. She is the first child in the family, and she suffers because she feels Willie replaced her in her father's affection. When she was young, her father had showered Emma with affection and attention, often taking her to his office. But, she remembers, "That was before he talked about nothing but *my boy* this and *my boy* that, after Willie was born" (*Nobody's Family*, 176). Here we see the seeds of Emma's interest in law as well as of her self-hatred. Her father implies that she is not good enough to follow in his footsteps because she is a girl.

Fitzhugh's attack on the destructiveness of traditional sex roles is obvious, but not simpleminded. The point is not simply that girls should be allowed to be lawyers and boys to be dancers, but rather that by denying them their aspirations, we may invalidate their sense of worth or the very essence of who they know themselves to be. In the Sheridan family, Emma resembles her father; Willie, his mother. Emma has her father's mind, laugh, and need to control. Willie takes after his mother's father and brother, with all of their natural talent for dancing and very little of his father's and Emma's ability in school. For the Sheridan children, the result of sex-role socialization is, therefore, serious psychological damage, but for Emma this is much more severe than for Willie.

He escapes psychological scarring, to some extent, because he is not as bright as Emma. She understands the frightening implications of her parents' expectations and behavior. He only knows that he must dance no matter what his parents say. More important, though, as I have already noted, is that Willie's uncle supports his desire to dance and his mother eventually does, too. In contrast, Mrs. Sheridan will not support Emma's desire to be a lawyer. As her husband wants Willie to become just like him, she wants Emma to become just like her. So conditioned by her early childhood experiences with her father and genetically determined to be like him, Emma is rejected by both parents because of who she is. The result, as she eventually realizes, is that she rejects herself. She is a loser—in life and in her dreams. Wanting what she can't have, her parents' acceptance of and appreciation for her, she relies on food and fantasy to fulfill her needs, but they only make her fat and isolated. They do not provide her with what she desires, but rather ensure that she is a loser. When she asks herself why she chooses to lose, her answer is that she does so because she wants to please her parents and to make them love her (*Nobody's Family*, 205–212).

Although becoming a loser may not seem the logical result of a desire to please and win love, Emma's reasoning is flawless. She recognizes that her becoming a successful lawyer will never please her father or mother because it will upset their beliefs about what is and what ought to be, which explains why Willie's taking the job on Broadway distresses her father even after he has given in to his wife's insistence that Willie be allowed to do so. Her father does not want his wife to violate his expectations any more than he wants Willie to do so. The only way Emma can be herself and please her parents, therefore, is to be a loser. Both parents believe that females who are independent and intelligent and unmarried will inevitably be unhappy. Emma's efforts to change the situation, moreover, are also misdirected. Because she wants her parents to love her—that is, value her for who she is— she tries to change them. She tries to persuade them that it is all right for men to be dancers and for women to be lawyers. Eventually, she realizes that she cannot change them because a person can change only herself or himself.

This realization, however, is a very angry one. Although it may very well allow her to save herself from continued overeating and fantasizing, it also requires that she relinquish all desire for her parents' approval and love, and it leads her to reject them as well as their beliefs. She turns to her peers for support, instead, knowing that the similar familial experiences of Sanders, Goldin, and Ketchum will allow them to understand her past need to please her parents and her current need to change in order to please herself.

To a large extent, Emma's rejection of her parents and affirmation of herself, like Harriet's growth in empathy, can be seen as the result of the shift in cognition that characteristically begins around 11 years of age. The individuation process requires that adolescents separate from their parents, and this separation often involves an initial, rather wholesale rejection of parental values. The more difficult the separation (usually due to intense identification with one of the parents or to a substantial lack of self-esteem), the more thoroughgoing the rejection. Emma's rather total condemnation of her parents is, therefore, understandable and believable.

Psychological Depth

But separation cannot be successfully achieved unless we eventually come to understand and forgive our parents. At some point as adults no longer dependent on our parents for self-esteem, we see why they responded to us as they did, we understand that they could not have behaved differently, given who they were, and we accept them as flawed human beings who did the best that they could. Once again, then, we are able to love them, now not as children needing to believe and expecting that they are everything we need them to be, but rather as adults recognizing that a parent can only be who she or he is regardless of what a child may need.

At 11, Emma has only begun to separate. Because doing so is new to her and because it will be very difficult for her, she cannot afford to feel any compassion for her parents. Her lack of charity clearly limits her as a narrator. In her first two novels, Fitzhugh provides a context whereby her heroine's viewpoint and behavior are contrasted with those of others, her heroine's strengths and limitations are revealed, and a wisdom greater than her heroine's is thereby made available. Yet nothing in this novel qualifies Emma's viewpoint and points out that her analysis of her situation is one-sided.

At 11, Emma is a very wise child. Indeed, we may question that at her age and in her situation, she would ever arrive at her final insights and thereby begin to save herself. A child as damaged as she is unlikely to get the necessary emotional distance from rejecting parents to perceive them as they are. Even if she does, she will find it extremely difficult, if not impossible, to love herself sufficiently to be herself and to give up wanting her parents to love her for who she is. The effort to do so will be a lifelong process, full of setbacks, if not doomed to failure. Fitzhugh herself never fully overcame the effects of her controlling father. Adults from such backgrounds seldom do. If they are very bright, like Fitzhugh and, perhaps, Emma, they may come to understand the complex dynamics of what happened to them during childhood, what the effects were on them, and what they must do to reverse these effects. But most will not begin to do so until they are young adults and even then not without professional help. Surely, therefore, we must suspect that Emma's understanding is Fitzhugh's and not really that of an emotionally deprived 11-year-old.

What's more, understanding and internalizing that understanding are two very different things. Fitzhugh wrote three books trying to embody and explain the truths that made her survival possible. In her intense insistence that self-love is essential to survival, she reveals how difficult it was to love herself when she had not been sufficiently loved as a child. Her very insistence is evidence of need. If she had loved herself easily and naturally, she would not have needed to emphasize the importance of self-love over and over again, even to the point of ignoring the importance of charity in *Nobody's Family Is Going to Change*.

To some extent, we may pardon this lapse, recognizing that children in Emma's position cannot afford compassion for their parents. Perhaps her personal experience led Fitzhugh to this recognition, perhaps Emma reflects Fitzhugh's awareness that her uncle was destroyed by his desire to please his parents, perhaps her desire to save children from the kind of suffering she experienced as a child led her to support and not qualify 11-year-old Emma's limited viewpoint, or perhaps her anger about what had happened to her as a child overwhelmed her capacity for forgiveness as she wrote this novel, prohibiting her from balancing the need for self-love with the need for charity, as she did in *Harriet the Spy* and *The Long Secret.* I suspect the last explanation may be the correct one. Both Beth Ellen and Harriet are happier versions of Fitzhugh than Emma is. Creating Emma and Willie, Fitzhugh isolated her anger, separated it from her primary source of joy and fulfillment, and gave each a life of its own. Willie, who is Fitzhugh's artistic side, expresses all the happiness she felt creating, but Emma, who is her anger, dominates the novel.

Whatever the case may be, *Nobody's Family Is Going to Change* lacks the psychological depth of Fitzhugh's earlier novels. Emma explains her family with true and complex understanding, but we must question that Emma would arrive at her eventual insights or that she would be able to act on them. Nor can we rest content that Emma's insights are as wise as those offered in *Harriet the Spy* and *The Long Secret.* Some children may profit by them. Some children may need very much to read them. But limited as they are, they reduce the stature of Fitzhugh's third novel.

Social Criticism

As I have already indicated, many critics have noted the emphasis on social criticism in *Nobody's Family Is Going to Change.* Certainly, Fitzhugh is a social critic in all of her novels but never as thoroughly so as in this one. What is immediately apparent is the number of social concerns Fitzhugh takes on: sexism, racism, obesity, physical and emotional child abuse, homosexuality, alcoholism, and poverty. What is perhaps not so immediately apparent is the underlying motive for her criticism. Nodelman points out that she attacks discrimination of any kind, but he fails to explore her reason. To be sure, he analyzes the negative effects of Mr. Sheridan's sexism and conventional "white" values on Emma, but without biographical information about Fitzhugh, he could not begin to understand the implications of her portrait of Emma.

Like Harriet and Beth Ellen, Emma is Fitzhugh. In Harriet, Fitzhugh portrayed the strong, sure side of herself that enabled her to write and paint. In Beth Ellen, she explored her fearfulness as a child and her transcendence of fear when she recognized her anger and affirmed her choice of art as a career. In Emma, she focused on her anger. The source of that anger was the isolation, insecurity, and fear she experienced as a child because her father lied to her about her mother's being dead and in many other ways failed to respect her individuality. That anger is the motive for Fitzhugh's attack on discrimination.

The biographical evidence suggests that as Fitzhugh became increasingly aware of how her childhood affected her, she also came to see her writing for children as a way to help children avoid growing up as she did. In an undated letter to Joan Williams, probably written in 1966 or 1967, Fitzhugh wrote, "Writing for children has given me a wonderful sense of *doing good*, which I guess I must feel. All other writing had become vanity to me, saying see-how-well-I-write, or worse of course, just writing badly."

In her children's books, her emphasis on self-love was one way to help, but so was her criticism of judging others inadequate or worthless on the basis of their sex, race, weight, sexual orientation, financial situation, choice of profession, or any other difference. She saw clearly that people used such judgments as a way of controlling others, especially children, teaching them to doubt themselves and to fear others. She saw that such judgments of children result in adults incapable of trust and intimacy. She wanted to teach children (and herself) to discount such judgments and instead to determine who they are (what makes them truly happy) and to develop their true selves with love and appreciation for their individuality. This motivation accounts for the energy and power of the book. Fitzhugh's own enormous anger drives her attack on discrimination.

In support of the biographical evidence is the primary emphasis on children's rights in this novel. Fitzhugh's creation of the Children's Army in *Nobody's Family* provides her with the means for this emphasis as well as for educating Emma about her family. Attending meetings of the Children's Army, Emma (and the reader) learns of the many ways in which adults harm children. The motto of the Children's Army, what's more, is the heart of every book Fitzhugh ever wrote: "Children come first" (*Nobody's Family*, 74). As a member of the Army explains to Emma, what this motto means is that children's welfare should be the basis for every decision adults make, for if it were, only good decisions would be made. Later the Army provides an additional motto to ponder: "INNER PROGRESS BEFORE OUTER PROGRESS" (*Nobody's Family*, 108). Emma and the three other girls who join up with her, Sanders, Goldin, and Ketchum, decide that this motto explains why adults make many bad decisions. Ignoring the advice of this motto, society recognizes the creation of buildings, highways, and machines as progress, and children are ignored and never grow up.

Taken together, these mottos form the essence of Fitzhugh's social criticism. Instead of rearing children who know who they are and who are proud of themselves, adults stress the importance of the external world for themselves and for their children. Not having grown up, they cannot help their children to do so, and the cycle continues. Eventually, Emma finds the Children's Army useless to her and Willie because they only intervene when parents are clearly breaking a law. Also the leader of the Children's Army, Harrison Carter, turns out to be a "male chauvinist pig," who does not believe that her father's refusal to accept Willie's and her career aspirations could ruin their lives. Indeed, he agrees with her father that they are poor choices because females should not practice law and males should not dance.

But before this meeting with Harrison, which leads to Emma's rejection of the Army, she meets with Sanders, Goldin, and Ketchum to discuss their mutual oppression. She agrees with Ketchum's statement that "whatever a person is, that's what he is, and a person wants to be the way he is" (*Nobody's Family*, 120), and she comes to understand that the failure to accept others for who they are results in efforts to change them, which is what all of their parents constantly work to do. Harrison Carter, who opposes physical abuse of children, refuses to see parents' attitudes as a serious problem for children, but in attempting to explain to him how parents ruin children by conditioning them to see themselves as their parents do, Emma moves toward the insight that allows her to change, and Fitzhugh emphasizes the potential tragedy of parents who do not allow their children self-determination and self-love.

Parents are not, however, simply the villains. Over Emma's shoulder, we see her parents clearly, if unsympathetically. In her struggle to save herself, she can—perhaps—not afford to feel any sympathy, but we can. William Sheridan, Sr., grew up in Bedford-Stuyvesant, one of Manhattan's worst slums. His mother dead and his father a drunk, he went to work at nine to support his brother and himself. He worked his way through law school, despite poverty, lack of sleep, and racism. Then he rescued his wife from a family supported by an alcoholic, seldom-working father. She, too, was motherless and responsible for raising a younger brother. Both parents, in other words, came from abusive families, which taught them not to trust others and forced them to grow up too fast. Both were too frightened as children to dare to be any more different than they already were as poor blacks. Both, therefore, aspired to white, middle-class social norms. Both learned to conform to and to control their environment as a means of security. They sought the possessions and status that would make them safe. Essentially, they clung together in fear, never developing the capacity for intimacy.

We may judge their choices and behavior as wrong, recognizing the high cost to their children and to them. They are, nevertheless, perfectly understandable, believable, and forgivable. As children, Mr. and Mrs. Sheridan were also victims. Their parents failed them even more severely than they fail their children. In other words, Fitzhugh shows that the horror of child abuse is that it is cyclical, repeated generation after generation. Whatever improvement there may be in parents' ability to care for their children in one generation, the elimination of the effects of parents' failures usually requires several generations and may never completely occur. Thus, Fitzhugh's intense desire to help children survive victimizing families. Thus, the sharp edge of social criticism in *Nobody's Family Is Going to Change.*

Conclusion

In the final analysis, Fitzhugh's third novel makes me sad. Her desperation is everywhere evident. Her intense needs to escape her past, to help children avoid being harmed by adults, to explain how it all might be different all show. But so does the impossibility of what she desires. Unfortunately, we must be *taught* to love ourselves and to trust others. Our experiences with our parents teach us how to be intimate, and it is questionable that we will ever develop these capacities unless our parents have them.

Like Fitzhugh, Emma finds it difficult to touch or be touched by another human being (see chapter 2, note 8). She mistrusts whoever or whatever attracts her. At the end of the novel, she is intensely angry with her parents. We can believe she will survive. She will probably lose weight and go to law school and one day be a successful lawyer. But will she be able to trust and love someone else? Will she ever be able to touch and be touched? Won't she always fear being consumed and rejected again, as she was by her parents? If she ever has children, what kind of parent will she be? Won't she repeat the cycle? Although certainly she will understand her children's needs better than her parents understood hers, she will not, just as none of us can, fully erase childhood scars.

The tragedy here is that we can understand better than we can live. We can know that we need to love ourselves and others, but as children, we are, nevertheless, dependent on others to give us the love that teaches us how to do so. Understanding what's wrong with our families, as Emma does, might allow us to change somewhat. It certainly would allow us to survive in some fashion. Emma learns how not to live. Rather than internalize her parents' rejection of who she is, she dismisses their opinions as their "problem, not mine" (*Nobody's Family,* 221). In effect, she does what her parents have taught her to do: she rejects those unlike herself. How will she learn to accept others for who they are? Who will teach her? Someone must if she is to learn, for this is not a lesson that can be learned alone.

The cycle of abuse thus continues in Emma and in Fitzhugh. Understanding is never sufficient. If it were, we would all be living the good life. Unfortunately, we are all imperfect. We may see what we need, but be blind to others' needs, as they may be blind to ours. Pointedly condemning our folly, ignorance, and cruelty and asserting what is necessary for the good life, the author of didactic literature runs the risk of forgetting human imperfection. The intelligence runs away with the heart. Anger prevails, when perhaps the wiser response is sorrow.

In *Nobody's Family Is Going to Change,* Fitzhugh allows Emma's anger to prevail. Fitzhugh here identifies with someone very like herself, as Harriet identifies with Harrison Withers, and fails to put herself in the shoes of those whom she portrays as the enemy, as Harriet fails to do with Marian Hawthorne, for example. Allowing Emma's point of view to control determines that her parents will seem villains. It also assures that child readers with families like Emma's will be offered clear guidance about how to survive emotional rejection with minimal damage to their self-esteem. Had Fitzhugh used another narrative method, this guidance might have been less available to children. Indeed, the novel might not have been a children's novel. Speculation about how she might or should have written the novel, however, is pointless. She chose not to qualify Emma's understanding of herself and her family and thereby created a clear lesson. Although the lesson reflects a complex knowledge of psychology and may be vital to some children's welfare, I think the price Fitzhugh paid to teach it was too high. For one thing, we may question Emma's being able to achieve her eventual insight and, therefore, fault Fitzhugh's realism. But most important, we must lament the view of humanity offered in the novel and recognize that compared to that of *Harriet the Spy* or of *The Long Secret,* it is simplistic.

6

Beth Ellen's Mistakes
as an Artist: *Sport*

Delacorte published Fitzhugh's last novel five years after her death. It is so different from her earlier novels that it has prompted critics to see it as unfinished and friends to wonder if Fitzhugh wrote it.[1] There can be no doubt, however, that she wrote at least some of the published version. According to Charlotte Zolotow, Fitzhugh submitted a draft of *Sport* to Harper & Row in the late sixties or early seventies. Although they were interested in publishing it if certain revisions were made, Fitzhugh withdrew the manuscript from consideration. Lois Morehead reports that it was found among her papers after her death by Carrie Ryan, an employee of Dell, and subsequently published under the editorship of Ron Buehl.

Although we cannot be sure of when the novel was written, we can narrow the possibilities by attending to the book's characteristics and to the events of Fitzhugh's life. The book begins at the end of the summer Harriet and Beth Ellen become friends and continues through Sport's first few weeks at a new school. Thus, it was intended as the third book of a trilogy about Harriet and her friends, allowing us to conclude that it was written after *Harriet the Spy* and *The Long Secret*. Knowing that Fitzhugh's father died at about the time of *The Long Secret*'s publication, that her stepmother died about two years later, and that this third novel focuses on Sport's grandfather's dying and death, we can surmise that she might have been working on *Sport* during the mid-sixties, but also that she might not have been able to complete or polish the manuscript until she had had some time to process her personal experiences. This sequence of events seems especially probable when we remember that *Bang, Bang, You're Dead* was written and published in the late sixties.

We can also guess that the amount of revision suggested by Harper led Fitzhugh to abandon the possibility of publication. *Sport* is a lightweight beside any of Fitzhugh's other novels and is very nearly the opposite of *Nobody's Family Is Going to Change*. It displays the same irreverence and zany sense of humor as *Harriet the Spy*. But rather than intellectual complexity, it offers a fast pace and melodramatic events and characters. It is a book as fully controlled by the emotions as *Nobody's Family Is Going to Change* is by the intellect.

Sport, or Simon Rocque, it turns out, is the grandson of a multimillionaire and the son of Charlotte Vane, a woman much like Beth Ellen's mother. Like Beth Ellen's cool and distant grandmother, Simon Vane loves his grandchild and despairs of his daughter, Charlotte. At his death, he leaves Sport all of his estate except for one fourth, which goes to his mother—unless she stays in the States and acts half-time as her son's trustee and parent, in which case, she gets half. (Sport's parents are divorced, and his father has custody half the time.) Hating children and desiring only her own pleasure, his mother is an entirely evil woman. Only one small piece of evidence might explain her selfishness—the comment that her father hated women and loved Sport because he was the son he never had (*Sport,* 84). But as motivation for her behavior, Simon Vane's misogyny is never developed, leaving us with a one-sided and finally unbelievable character. All of the Vanes are similarly undeveloped, as is Kate, the wonderful woman whom Sport's father Matthew marries. She is as perfect as Charlotte is imperfect. In addition, Harriet and Sport's other friends (one black, one Jewish, and one Chicano) here appear as types leaning toward caricatures. Only Sport and his father are developed with any complexity, and even Sport is less fully developed than are Harriet, Beth Ellen, or Emma in the other novels. What's more, the plot does not require Sport to grow as do the protagonists of Fitzhugh's other novels. Rather, it confronts him with others' craziness and meanness and portrays how he survives attempts to confine and abuse him. In all of this, his mother is the villain. Mostly, she ignores him and his desires. If he does not do as she wishes, she assaults him verbally or locks him in his room, once without food. Caring only for money and desiring all that her father left, she eventually kidnaps Sport and tries to prove his father unfit. Indeed, there are two kidnapping attempts in the book, and Sport and his friends foil both. The first time, his mother locks him up in a room in the Plaza Hotel, from which he escapes under a food server with the help of his Chicano friend, Chi Chi. The second time Chi Chi, his Jewish friend Seymour, and his black friend Harry save him from being dragged into the Vane limousine by his aunt, only to be interrupted by the police and accused of attacking the car. The book ends with his mother's departure for Europe and her renunciation of all but a fourth of the estate. Sport will thus live happily ever after, rich and at home in a loving family.

These melodramatic characters and lurid events are entertaining and satisfying, but they are mostly without psychological depth. They appeal to the heart and not to the head. We feel sorry for and proud of Sport; we hate and dismiss his mother. We never think about why either of them is the way they are. Cheering Sport on, we rest content that he ends up happy and that she is driven off alone to Europe. His cruel, unloving mother does not seriously affect him. She angers him, and he hates being with her. But he never despairs. Her dislike of or lack of interest in him never affects his opinion of himself. He, furthermore, acquires an ordinary, loving mother, who gives him all that he needs and desires. Sport gets what Fitzhugh wished she had had as a child. In allowing him to do so, however, Fitzhugh denies the inevitable results on a child of an unloving parent. She denies her own experience. Such denials are the excesses of the heart. They reveal Beth Ellen's mistakes as an artist, supporting her and readers' naive faith that if they are good, they will receive what they desire and live happily ever after. They stand in sharp contrast to all that Fitzhugh in her other novels says about the importance and development of self-love.

The Critics

On the whole, the reviewers have appreciated Fitzhugh's fourth novel for what it is. Few have dismissed the novel for its lack of realism. Only the reviews in *Language Arts* and *Publishers Weekly* rejected the novel wholesale, the first as "unbelievable," the second as "labored and mean spirited."[2] Others, even when troubled by stereotypes and melodrama, also saw and praised the resulting humor and pace. And the reviewers for *Book List, Best Sellers, New Yorker,* and *Childhood Education* praised *Sport* as a wild and hilariously funny farce, *Book List* going as far as to call it "a worthy successor to *Harriet the Spy.*"[3]

The reviews anticipate Nodelman's defense of the book as "fun simply because it is not subtle" (Nodelman, 141). Indeed, they reveal a general change in standards of realism in the children's book reviewing field since the sixties. Many of these reviewers obviously recognize that simple standards of realism are inadequate for judgment of this book and read it as a kind of satire— in this case, farce. Another reason for their praise, however, is that *Sport* is less aggressive, critical, and offensive than *Nobody's Family Is Going to Change.* Its attack on the rich is not likely to offend many, nor is its exposure of New York City police officers. Its portrait of ideal home life, moreover, softens all of its criticism.

Sport's Personality

The essentially positive critical response to *Sport* probably results largely from the nature of its protagonist. Of all of Fitzhugh's protagonists, Sport is the most likeable. He is the least critical of others and the most ordinary. Like most other boys, he likes sports and comics. Like a few, he wants to be an accountant when he grows up. He is most unusual in his role as parent for his absentminded father. Matthew Rocque cannot keep track of time, money, or much else. As a writer, he lives mostly in another world—the one he is currently writing about. He loves his son, but he also relies on him to take care of the details of their lives— the cleaning, cooking, scheduling, and budgeting. Sport recognizes and accepts his father's flaws. He perceives them not as monstrous, but rather as inevitable. In other words, as Sport sees it, Matthew Rocque was simply born a writer and, thereby, lacks most of the abilities required of a good parent. Similarly, Sport, we are led to believe, was born with some of these abilities. Like his grandfather, who in the course of a lifetime earned $30 million, Sport seems gifted with management skills and money sense. By nature, he is a better parent (at least in these areas) than his father.

Nevertheless, the reader feels sorry for Sport because he must worry about money and household matters. No one believes that a child should have to be responsible for a parent. It is easy to feel that the Sport we see in *Harriet the Spy,* fearing poverty and chaos, maintains what security he has by keeping house and financial records. In *Sport,* Fitzhugh gives us reason for believing that Sport would enjoy his role as parent, that is, he is by genetic inheritance naturally adept with money and management. Still, even if we admire Sport, we feel sorry for him. When Kate appears on the scene and takes over as parent, the reader becomes acutely aware of what Sport has been missing—peace of mind and enough to eat. The eating scenes are almost too much. The loving description of every item of the meals Kate prepares, as well as of other meals Sport eats, occupies much space in the novel. The result is that the novel appeals to child readers who have hit a growth spurt and are preoccupied with food, but it is also that we see what Sport was missing before Kate's arrival.

But if we feel sorry for Sport because his father is an inadequate parent, we feel even more so because his mother is a monstrous one. The scenes with his mother balance those with Kate, heightening our sense of them as opposites. Kate cares for him; his mother, only for herself. Kate feeds him; his mother sends him to bed without dinner. Kate frees him; his mother confines him to his room at her home, kidnaps him, and locks him in a room at the Plaza Hotel. Kate invites his friends to her wedding party; his mother insists his friends are unfit. The one is too good to be true; the other, too bad. The one is what every child desires; the other, what every child fears. They are fairy-tale characters, expressing universal emotions about parents. Certainly, Charlotte Vane is another version of the bad parent, usually a bad mother, who haunted Fitzhugh's life and who haunts her books. In any case, her presence in Sport's life increases our sympathy for him. Indeed, as is true of all fairy tales, we are so busy worrying about how the hero will escape the clutches of this evil woman that we never stop to think much about what sort of person he is.

When we do, though, we see a kind, generous, loving person— a Cinderella figure. He is always doing for others. Even when he visits his friend, Seymour O'Neil (his father was Irish), he works in the family's candy store to help out Mrs. O'Neil. In addition, Sport is without bigotry or selfishness. His mother's anti-Semitic comments outrage him, as do the assumptions of the police officers that he and his friends are juvenile delinquents because they are not from white, middle-class homes. Unlike both Harriet and Beth Ellen, however, Sport is critical of others only when he is directly a victim of their behavior. Even then, he has little time or opportunity for reflection and analysis. He is much too busy surviving. The result is a character most readers will like.

The Artist

Like all of Fitzhugh's other work for children, *Sport* offers us a portrait of the artist. Matthew Rocque, however, is not as central to *Sport* as are any of the other artist characters to their respective novels, although he exhibits many of the same characteristics. A man who loves his work and his son, Matthew Rocque is still a child in spirit. Like all of Fitzhugh's other artists, he is a positive character, even if he is an inadequate parent. Little more can be said of him or of Fitzhugh's exploration of the artist in this novel. The focus of *Sport* is rather on the child's need for good parents and a loving, secure home, and, important as this focus is, it does not allow Fitzhugh room for achieving the intellectual depth characteristic of her other novels.

As we have already seen in examining *Nobody's Family Is Going to Change,* Fitzhugh's focus seems to have shifted after finishing *The Long Secret.* Her attention to the artist is less central in her last two novels than in her first two. Rather, she emphasizes various forms of parental abuse resulting from a failure to accept one's children for who they are, which is, of course, a major theme in all of her work. This shift in focus suggests that emotionally she had come to terms with herself as a writer and a painter. At least, she seems to have found it less necessary to defend artists than she did in her earlier work.

One other fact suggests her increased self-acceptance. In both of her last novels, Fitzhugh used her own nicknames as names for her boy protagonists. Her friend Lois Morehead called her Willie, and her friend Marianne Meaker called her Sport. The character Willie is both child and artist and thereby allows Fitzhugh to explore again the joy, self-absorption, and obsessiveness of the child artist as well as parents' failure to understand such a child. Still, with the exception of Willie's father, everyone loves Willie's dancing. Sport accepts and loves his artist father as he is. Equally important, although Matthew Rocque displays all of the self-absorption characteristic of the artist and its effects on his son are evident, the novel in no way suggests that the artist could or should be different. One conflict that powers Fitzhugh's other books is thus absent here.

Farce

Like Fitzhugh's other work, *Sport* is satiric, but it is better described as farce. Rather than rely on characterization or plot, it presents exaggerated, improbable situations, its humor arising from gross incongruities, coarse wit, or horseplay. It is a wildly funny book, largely because its outrageous and fast-paced scenes read like a series of comic set pieces: for example, driving with Mr. Rocque through the streets of New York at 50 miles an hour; eating everything in sight the first night Kate cooks; and shopping with Sport's mom at Brooks Brothers, where she buys him a whole year's wardrobe in under an hour. There are also the following three memorable scenes: the last time Sport sees his grandfather alive—the nurse yelling, his mother glaring, his grandfather's hand creeping toward Sport; his grandfather's funeral, during which everything is done with absolute correctness and no feeling; and finally, the visit by his friends to his mother's house—Harriet obsessively taking notes, Seymour agreeing effusively to everything, and Harry speaking of himself as "plain American nigger" in a cultivated British accent. Much of what happens is slapstick, involving, for example, speeding cars, dunked old women, overeating, thrown shoes, someone being dragged into a car, and an escape under a serving cart. There is no time for analysis by Sport or the reader. Sport is too busy saving himself, and the reader is too busy laughing.

The book rests on and develops a series of gross incongruities. On one side, there are home (in the form of the apartment), Sport's dad, Kate, Sport's friends, school, and neighborhood. On the opposite side, there are his grandfather's house, his mother, his Aunt Carrie, the Plaza Hotel, Brooks Brothers, restaurants, bars, limousines, a variety of servants and employees, and the police. The contrasts are stark—of Kate and Charlotte, but also of Charlotte and her father, of Sport's father and mother, of his father and Kate, of Seymour and Harry, of Beth Ellen and Harriet, and so forth. Besides the characters, the settings are similarly opposed—poor and rich, small and large, crammed and empty, happy and miserable. So are the events. The essential event at home is Sport's father's falling in love. It results in a courtship, Kate's visits to their apartment, a marriage, a wedding party, and a good mother's care for Sport. The essential event in the other world is Sport's grandfather's illness. It results in Sport's mother's return from Europe, a deathbed scene, his grandfather's eventual death, a funeral, Sport's inheritance, and a bad mother's abuse of Sport.

The two sides or worlds, in other words, are absolute opposites, as Northrop Frye says they always are in romance.[4] We see the same patterning of contrasts in *Nobody's Family Is Going to Change.* The difference between the two lies in the emphasis of *Sport* on plot (characteristic of farce and most romance) as compared to that of *Nobody's Family Is Going to Change* on character (characteristic of psychological realism and some satire). In *Sport* we participate in literal love and death; in *Nobody's Family Is Going to Change,* we experience symbolic or psychological love and death—that is, love and death of the self in response to parents' attitudes toward their children. *Sport,* consequently, moves much faster than does *Nobody's Family Is Going to Change.* Its gross incongruities and fast pace (central to farce) make us laugh, provoke our deepest fears, and satisfy our deepest longings. They also move the book closer to the realm of fairy tale or fantasy than any of Fitzhugh's other novels.

Social Criticism

Also different is the limited extent to which *Sport* offers social criticism. It makes fun of rich people who care only for their own immediate pleasure. It condemns parents who do not care for their children. It makes fun of the police or of anyone who judges a person on the basis of his color or possessions. It has a bit to say about death, divorce, remarriage, and stepparents.

The scene involving the police officer who wants to arrest Sport and his friends for attacking the Vane limousine, when, in fact, his friends had helped Sport escape being kidnapped by his aunt, is the angriest one in the novel, condemning the New York City Police for their racist and classist assumptions. The times when his mother reveals her bigotry run close seconds to this one. Offsetting others' bigotry is the fact that Sport's friends are of different racial or ethnic backgrounds. Thus, the novel promotes cultural diversity—if the friends do not seem so stereotypical that they are dismissed as unrealistic.

Besides the discrimination that characterizes American life, Fitzhugh also looks at some other topics often introduced to children by means of fiction. One of these is death. That Charlotte and Carrie do all the right things for their father's funeral, including an extended period of mourning afterward, and feel no grief criticizes false attitudes toward death, in contrast to Sport's genuine, if low-key, grief and his relatively quick return to activities he enjoys. Fitzhugh also provides a positive view of remarriage and stepmothers.

Beyond these scenes, there is very little that counts as social criticism, and even Fitzhugh's consideration of bad parents, death, remarriage, and stepmothers seems more intended to advance the plot than to add to the satire. The urge to criticize is muted here, amazingly so when one thinks of Fitzhugh's other books, particularly *Nobody's Family Is Going to Change,* which was written after *Sport.* Even Fitzhugh's central themes get lost in the rapid pace and the thin characterization. We have already noted that the novel has little to say about the artist, focusing instead on Sport's relationships with his parents. But what the novel implies about parent/child relationships is too obvious and superficial to be of much value. Characters are either too good or too bad. Rather than trace the effects of events on them, Fitzhugh moves them pell-mell from one event to another.

Conclusion

Among Fitzhugh's work, her last novel is, indeed, a "sport." It is remarkably unlike any of her other published work. We could conclude that it is simply unfinished. But we might also see it as an expression of another side of this complex writer.

Sport expresses, denies, and/or resolves all of the concerns that drive Fitzhugh's writing. It is wish-fulfillment fantasy. Bad parents are replaced by good parents. Abundance and comfort rescue the hero from poverty and want. He escapes unscathed from all of the horrors of Fitzhugh's childhood. His adventures are funny and, ultimately, happy. Even in the hero's worst moments, the reader can expect him to succeed in getting what he wants. Certainly, *Sport* must have been cathartic for Fitzhugh to write. Perhaps it reflects her state of mind in the late sixties, when she no longer needed to worry about pleasing her father and stepmother and after she had received her considerable inheritance. Perhaps it reflects her need to deny her family's continuing effect on her and her sense of loss at their deaths. Such denial was not possible in her next novel. Her struggle to explain a rejecting family's effect on a child and the child's consequent sense of loss dominates *Nobody's Family Is Going to Change*.

In any case, *Sport* is one of a kind among Fitzhugh's work. It is also much loved by children, who have as much fun and joy in reading it as Fitzhugh may very well have had in writing it.

7

The Contribution of the Artist:
Fitzhugh's Importance and Influence

Fitzhugh's Works

There may be future publications of manuscripts found among
Fitzhugh's papers after her death. There may be future dramati-
zations of her work, such as the Broadway production and after-
school special both called *The Tap Dance Kid* and the Children's
Theatre production of *Harriet the Spy.* Although it is impossible
to predict what these publications and productions might be like
without having read through the papers she left or without knowing who will do the productions, those to date have not added
substantially to Fitzhugh's reputation. *Sport* and the picture
books published, as well as the dramatic adaptations of *Nobody's
Family Is Going to Change* and of *Harriet the Spy,* are light-
weights when compared to the three novels Fitzhugh saw through
the publication process, especially *Harriet the Spy.* They are very
unlike her other work.[1] One might assume that any further publications or productions would be similar.[2]

In any case, we can assess Fitzhugh's importance to and influence on children's literature only on the basis of what is now in
the public domain. That is a small number of books: four novels

and five picture books, and four of the nine were posthumously published. Moreover, only *Harriet the Spy* has received much critical attention.

Milestone/Masterpiece

It is widely accepted that *Harriet the Spy* is a milestone of children's literature. A forerunner of the "new realism," it paved the way for all those taboo-breaking children's books that were to appear in the sixties and seventies. Adults have given it no prizes for excellence. Indeed, upon its publication, many reviewers criticized it severely. They found the novel's negative portraits of adults, its failure to censure Harriet's spying and her critical attitude, and Ole Golly's advice that "sometimes you have to lie" troublesome. Today the novel seems mild compared with some of its followers, for example, S. E. Hinton's *The Outsiders* (1967), Paul Zindel's *The Pigman* (1968), Norma Klein's *Mom, the Wolf Man, and Me* (1972), Sandra Scoppetone's *Trying Hard to Hear You* (1974), and Robert Cormier's *After the First Death* (1979).[3] These books portray gang warfare, the manipulation and death of an old man, a single parent and a live-in boyfriend, a disastrous homosexual relationship between two adolescent males, and a teenage terrorist who is a trained, ruthless killer. Beside them, *Harriet the Spy* no longer even seems contemporary. The price of egg creams, the safety of the East Side of New York, and Harriet's innocence—all of these place the book in the mid-sixties. Nevertheless, it was a groundbreaking book in its time.

The history of this novel's reception is, in fact, an interesting example of the process whereby a book becomes part of the literary canon. As the discussion of its reviews here and in chapters 1 and 3 reveals, the novel threatened the children's literature establishment. It was different. It presented children and adults in ways contrary to the norm, for example, the way characters are presented in Eleanor Estes's *Moffat* series.[4] The three highly praised *Moffat* books portray a family of poor, good-hearted children, carefully nurtured by all of the adults in their small hometown. Boys are boys, girls are girls, parents take care of their children, and teachers and police are trustworthy and admirable. In the seventies, as the "new realism" took over the field, Estes's work lost its critical reputation, but in the fifties and early sixties, it was very highly thought of. By the mid-sixties, the shift was beginning to occur. Indeed, although Estes's *Ginger Pye*[5] won the Newbery award in 1952, a book she published the same year as *Harriet the Spy*—*The Alley*—received mixed reviews.[6] In other words, although most adults were not yet ready to accept a children's book as radically new as *Harriet,* many were also no longer satisfied with the safe, sweet world of the Estes books.

Times were changing. The civil rights movement, the protest against the Viet Nam War, the beginnings of the women's movement, or as many have called it, the rise of the "me" generation occurred in the sixties and seventies. Social unrest characterized these two decades. The conservative, traditional old ways and values were challenged on every side. Into this milieu came *Harriet the Spy,* a book that reflects social dissatisfaction and that promotes the rights of the individual—a book that spoke to the time. So gradually the book gained the acceptance and respect of adults.

But there is another reason why *Harriet the Spy* survived, probably the most important reason. Children loved it. While adults debated with one another about its value, children read it avidly and passed it on to their friends. It has been a perennial bestseller since its publication. In 1967, it came out in paper-back and received its only award, the Sequoyah Award, which is given each year by the children of Oklahoma. Adults worried about the book's popularity with children. In my hometown, there was talk of the rash of window peeping that broke out after each successive third-grade class read the book over a period of five years. Despite such worry, there is no doubt that children's delight in the book then and now has kept it alive.

Meanwhile, the times did change, and because *Harriet the Spy* had been popular with children, it was still around when adults began to value children's books with its honesty and themes. Ten years after its publication, my first piece about the book praised it for exactly these reasons. I celebrated its emphasis on the importance of individuality and self-love as the necessary foundation of any other kind of love. In exploring its themes and structure, I attempted to disassociate it from the thin, sensational examples of the "new realism" that followed it. I was concerned to identify it as more than a milestone—indeed, as a masterpiece. *Harriet* continued to gain in reputation as critics further explored and better understood it. Nodelman recognized it as satire and assisted other critics of children's literature to abandon the standards of realism as proof of literary success or failure. Bosmajian, exploring it as a study in alienation, spoke of the limits of individuality as an ideal and rejected the seventies' "cult of self," as so many have during the eighties. Paul celebrated it for its portrait of Harriet as a feminist writer. In other words, *Harriet the Spy* has rewarded extended study, and this, too, enables its survival. It might remain popular for a long time and then disappear. But when a book is amenable to multiple interpretations, especially to ones that reflect or support new cultural perceptions, it becomes part of the canon of children's literature, and its survival becomes nearly certain—even should it fail to remain popular.[7] For the culture will continue to change, and the book may very well decrease in popularity. But, to the extent that it is perceived as canonical, it will endure. As Barbara Herrnstein Smith explains, "Nothing endures like endurance" (Smith, 33), which is to say that "in addition to whatever various and perhaps continuously differing functions a work performs for succeeding generations of individual subjects, it will also begin to perform certain characteristic cultural functions by virtue of the very fact that it has endured" (Smith, 32). Other writers will begin to imitate it, and it will begin to "shape and create the culture in which its value is produced and transmitted and, for that very reason, to perpetuate the conditions of its own flourishing" (Smith, 32–33).

All the evidence at this time suggests that *Harriet the Spy* will endure. It still seems a remarkably funny and intellectually subtle piece of literature, a masterpiece. Many of its features (its antihero, its social criticism, its startling bluntness) have been imitated. The Judy Blume[8] books are obvious imitations of many of its more superficial characteristics, especially of the humor that results when an innocent child's honesty reveals adults' flaws. Indeed, today there are many, many children's books whose heroines are nontraditional, whose child characters are more egocentric than altruistic, whose events present the less savory side of American life and criticize Western culture, and whose focus is on girls as writers. All of these can be seen as direct descendents of *Harriet the Spy*. Unlike it, however, very few have been valorized by critical explication and evaluation. *Harriet* has thus far stood the test of time, that is, critics have continued to find its language and meaning relevant—if for different, even opposite, reasons. This book about Louise Fitzhugh offers new and different reasons why *Harriet the Spy* and perhaps other books by Fitzhugh belong in the canon of children's literature. Fitzhugh's work is especially rewarding when studied for what it has to say about the artist. Such an approach yields insights about various cultural perceptions of the artist and about Fitzhugh herself— who she was and why she wrote children's books.

Künstlerromane

In many ways, Fitzhugh's assumptions about the artist are romantic. Her artists are always childlike, indeed, usually children. At their best, they are enormously egocentric but apt in their perception of reality. They are also extreme individualists and, therefore, outsiders. Society makes them pay for their differences, which, in turn, makes them avid social critics.

On the other hand, much about Fitzhugh's portrait of the artist is modern, the psychological focus, in particular. None of Fitzhugh's artists truly choose their professions. Rather, as children, they simply become what they are—a writer, an artist, a dancer. Their families' failure to understand them forces them to be outsiders. It is not a stance they choose, and it causes them enormous pain. Their predispositions to become artists, in other words, are so strong that despite all opposition and the consequent unhappiness, they pursue what seems to be their destined means of expression. It is, in fact, their great joy in this means of expression that they cannot deny. Harriet's hand races across the page releasing her thoughts, Harrison gazes dreamily at his bird cage, Beth Ellen feels aglow as she announces she will be an artist, Willie's feet simply tap dance wherever he goes, and Sport's father lives in the fictional world he creates even while not writing.

Especially interesting is Fitzhugh's recognition of how confining traditional sex roles have been to the artist. As noted in the discussion of *Harriet the Spy,* Fitzhugh anticipated the portrait of the female artist as described by Linda Huf. Although, quite naturally, Fitzhugh was most interested in the female artist's need to throw off traditional sex-role conditioning, she also gave us Willie, whose nontraditional choice of tap dancing upsets his father. Still, Harriet and Beth Ellen are Fitzhugh's most insightful portraits of the artist, perhaps because they are clearly autobiographical.

Contribution

Fitzhugh's work, especially *Harriet the Spy* and *The Long Secret,* is important because it evocatively tells Fitzhugh's story and, by implication, the story of others who were like her as children. Essentially, this is a nontraditional girl's story. To the extent that it is set in a world that fosters traditional sex roles, it is also an angry story. For, as all of Fitzhugh's books reveal, a society that denies individual identity and indiscriminately supports conformity creates unhappy, imitative people—people who are more dead than alive. Beth Ellen is Fitzhugh's most convincing example. As a child with enormous potential—with talent as both a writer and a painter—Beth Ellen hides her true self out of fear of rejection. The result is a "mouse"—a quiet, withdrawn, bored, and boring child who is secretly consumed by anger. In the artist, as a character and as a self-portrait, Fitzhugh presents the opposite kind of character. Harriet is her most compelling example. Energetic, constantly thinking and moving, joyful, Harriet is fully alive until her mother prohibits her writing, at which point she becomes hostile and aggressive.

Clearly, Fitzhugh's primary message is that denial of one's essential self is destructive—of the individual and of the society. But just as clearly, Fitzhugh shows that unfettered egocentricity, such as Harriet's, isolates the individual. To say the least, others find it uncomfortable to be around her, and she is so limited in her understanding of others that she finds it difficult to bond with anyone, even as writer to reader. Just as Beth Ellen needs to care for herself, then, Harriet needs to care for others. The key is balance or harmony between the needs for identity and intimacy—between what Althea Horner calls "being and loving."[9]

Fitzhugh never really achieved such balance in her work. *Harriet the Spy* represents one side; *The Long Secret,* its opposite. *Nobody's Family Is Going to Change* extends the side represented by *Harriet the Spy.* It demonstrates why it is better to be like Harriet rather than like Beth Ellen, but it never explores the risks of being like Harriet. Caring for others, Emma nearly destroys herself; when she begins to care for herself, she has a chance at survival. *Sport* extends the side represented by *The Long Secret.* It demonstrates why it is better to be like Beth Ellen rather than Harriet, but it never explores the risks of being like Beth Ellen. Caring for others, Sport gets what he wants—abundant love and security. Denying truths evident in *Harriet the Spy* and *The Long Secret, Nobody's Family Is Going to Change* and *Sport* are extremes. When looked at in the context of all Fitzhugh's work, they clarify the extent to which Fitzhugh opposed love of self and love of others.

At any moment in an individual's life, self may be more important than others or vice versa. Horner and many other contemporary psychologists believe that over the course of a life, balance must occur if the person is to be happy and that if it does not, a person will exist in nearly total isolation or total conformity. The individualist gives up intimacy. The conformist gives up identity. To love, one must love oneself. To love oneself, one must love and be loved. It is not an either/or situation. One is not possible without the other.

Fitzhugh acknowledges these truths in her best work. Although *Harriet the Spy* emphasizes love of self, its protagonist's flaws are evident. In *The Long Secret,* Harriet's flaws are glaring, as Fitzhugh explores reasons why one might neglect self for others. Both novels finally show that self-love is the necessary beginning, the root from which love of others must grow, and both show that someone's love for the child is the source of her self-love. Both novels recognize the seamlessness of love.

Cost

Even though two of Fitzhugh's novels manage to transcend the conflict between self-love and love of others, it was, nevertheless, her obsession. Forced to choose between herself and her family during early childhood, she never recovered the cost of her choice. Without the easy ability to be intimate that comes with growing up in a loving family, she suffered emotionally throughout her life. She needed and never had a mother. She needed and never had an accepting family. On the other hand, she loved her work and thereby came to love herself as an artist. Others also came to love her as she was. She survived the emotional deprivation of her childhood—but not without scars. As often as not, her work speaks of the scars rather than the survival. But at its best, it speaks of both, allowing Fitzhugh and her readers to understand what happened to her as a child and what happens to all children who manage to survive despite having parents who do not sufficiently love them.

For, finally, the failure to accept a child is not to love sufficiently and to damage the child. No matter how hard the child may attempt to reject her family and to save herself, a sense of loss and inadequacy will persist. She may survive, but she will never easily love or be loved. She may crave love, but she will also fear the loss of self that accompanies it. In all likelihood, she will spend her life, as Louise Fitzhugh did, in search of and very nearly unable to accept the love she desperately needs. Paying such a price may result in some exceptional art, but I am not sure the art is ever adequate compensation for what it costs the artist.

Had Fitzhugh's family been able to accept her for who she was—nontraditional, female, artistic, gay—she would undoubtedly have grown up differently, and surely she would have told a different story. But they did not accept her, and, consequently, the story she told was the lonely one of the artist whose joy in self-expression allows for survival even when others reject her. Anthony Storr's *Solitude* suggests that this story is as valuable as any story about love. His book's thesis is that although many creative people have been solitary, it is "nonsense to suppose that they were necessarily unhappy or neurotic" (Storr, 201). He argues that individuals may "turn predominantly toward others or toward solitude to find the meaning of their lives" and that "some of the most profound and healing psychological experiences which individuals encounter take place internally, and are only distantly related, if at all, to interaction with other human beings" (Storr, 202). But Storr, like Horner, concludes that "the happiest lives are probably those in which neither interpersonal relationships nor impersonal interests are idealized as the only way to salvation. The desire and pursuit of the whole must comprehend both aspects of human nature" (Storr, 202).

Despite its humor and truth, Fitzhugh's is a sad story that I wish no one ever had to tell. We are, nevertheless, lucky that Louise Fitzhugh was there to tell it, because now we have her story for all those children who need to hear it.

Notes and References

Preface

1. Perry Nodelman, "Louise Fitzhugh," in *American Writers for Children since 1960*, ed. Glenn E. Estes, *Dictionary of Literary Biography*, vol. 52 (Detroit: Gale, 1986), 133–42; hereafter cited in text as Nodelman.
2. Werner Heisenberg, *The Physicist's Conception of Nature*, trans. Arnold J. Pomerans (New York: Harcourt, Brace & World, 1958).
3. Anthony Storr, *Solitude* (New York: Ballantine Books, 1988); hereafter cited in the text as Storr.

Chapter One

1. For information about female artistic development, see Sandra M. Gilbert and Susan Gubar, *The Madwoman in the Attic: The Woman Writer and the Nineteenth-Century Imagination* (New Haven, Conn.: Yale University Press, 1979); Lawrence J. Hatterer, M.D., "The Woman Artist," in *The Artist in Society: Problems and Treatment of the Creative Personality* (New York: Grove Press, 1965), 172–78; Elaine Hedges and Ingrid Wendt, eds., *In Her Own Image: Women Working in the Arts* (Old Westbury, N.Y.: Feminist Press, 1980); Mary Hiatt, *The Way Women Write* (New York: Columbia University Teachers College Press, 1977); Linda Huf, *A Portrait of the Artist as a Young Woman: The Writer as Heroine in American Literature* (New York: Frederick Ungar, 1983), hereafter cited in the text as Huf. For information about homosexual development, see Alan Bell, Martin Weinberg, and Sue Hammersmith, *Sexual Preference: Its Development in Men and Women* (Bloomington: Indiana University Press, 1981); Merle Miller, *On Being Different: What It Means to Be Homosexual* (New York: Random House, 1971); and Judd Marmor, ed., *Homosexual Behavior: A Modern Reappraisal* (New York: Basic Books, 1980). For information about satirists, see Leonard Feinberg, *The Satirist: His Temperament, Motivation, and Influence* (Ames: Iowa State University University Press, 1963). My understanding of writers for children evolves out of years of reading about their lives.

135

2. For example, Herbert Read, *Art and Alienation: The Role of the Artist in Society* (New York: Horizon Press, 1967; Hatterer, *The Artist in Society: Problems and Treatment of the Creative Personality*; Frank Barron, *Creative Person and Creative Process* (New York: Holt, Rinehart & Winston, 1969); and Ross Mooney and Taher Razik, eds., *Explorations in Creativity* (New York: Harper & Row, 1967).

3. Gilbert Highet, *The Anatomy of Satire* (Princeton, N.J.: Princeton University Press, 1962), 19–20, 238–41.

4. See Feinberg, *The Satirist,* 353–55, especially where he summarizes his argument for "an innate or early developed *talent for distortion*" in the satirist. See also chapter 8, "Development," where he speaks of a pattern of development: "Early evidence of satiric temperament; a relatively happy period during which mild and restrained satire is written; a disturbance; a return, with a vengeance, to the earlier caustic tone" (224).

5. Jerome Hamilton Buckley, *Seasons of Youth: The Bildungsroman from Dickens to Golding* (Cambridge: Harvard University Press, 1974), vii; hereafter cited in the text as Buckley.

6. *Bang, Bang, You're Dead,* with Sandra Scoppetone (New York: Harper & Row, 1969).

7. *Suzuki Beane,* with Sandra Scoppetone (New York: Doubleday, 1961).

8. *Harriet the Spy* (New York: Harper & Row, 1964), hereafter cited in the text as *Harriet*; and *The Long Secret* (New York: Harper & Row, 1965), hereafter cited in the text as *Long Secret.*

9. *Nobody's Family Is Going to Change* (New York: Farrar, Straus & Giroux, 1974); hereafter cited in the text as *Nobody's Family.*

10. *Sport* (New York: Delacorte, 1979); hereafter cited in the text as *Sport.*

11. *I Am Three,* illus. Susanna Natti (New York: Delacorte, 1982); *I Am Four,* illus. Susan Bonner (New York: Delacorte, 1982); *I Am Five* (New York: Delacorte, 1978).

12. Fitzhugh typically used the names and places and events of her life in her fiction; here the last name of the family is that of her friend Barbara Phelan.

13. Paul Binding, *Lorca: The Gay Imagination* (London: GMP, 1985), 190; hereafter cited in the text as Binding.

14. Robert K. Martin, *The Homosexual Tradition in American Poetry* (Austin: University of Texas Press, 1979), hereafter cited in the text as Martin; Emmanuel Cooper, *The Sexual Perspective: Homosexuality and Art in the Last One Hundred Years* (Indianapolis: Bobbs-Merrill, 1977); and Roger Austen, *Playing the Game: The Homosexual Novel in America* (Indianapolis: Bobbs-Merrill, 1977).

15. Maurice Beebe, *Ivory Towers and Sacred Founts: The Artist as*

Hero in Fiction from Goethe to Joyce (New York: New York University Press, 1964), 5–6; hereafter cited in the text as Beebe.

16. Review of Louise Fitzhugh's show at the Banfer Gallery (8–25 May 1963), *Art News* 62 (May 1963): 65.

17. Irene Zahava, ed., *The Second WomanSleuth Anthology: Contemporary Mystery Stories by Women* (Freedom, Calif.: Crossing Press, 1989; hereafter cited in the text as Zahava.

18. Review of *Nobody's Family Is Going to Change, Publishers Weekly*, 4 November 1974, 68.

19. *The Tap Dance Kid*, written and directed by Barra Grant, music by John Morris, produced by Evelyn Barron (New York: Learning Corp., 1978), and *The Tap Dance Kid,* musical based on the novel *Nobody's Family Is Going to Change,* book by Charles Blackwell, music by Henry Krieger, lyrics by Robert Lorick, produced by Evelyn Barron, Harvey J. Klaris, and Michel Stuart (Broadhurst Theater, New York, 21 December 1983).

20. "Harriet the Spy," adapted by Leslie Brody, directed by Kyle Donnelly (Children's Theatre, Minneapolis, 5 February to 2 April 1988).

Chapter Two

1. Charlotte Zolotow first told me that Mrs. Morehead withdrew this manuscript, which Ms. Zolotow considers a fine piece; Mrs. Morehead says she withdrew the manuscript because she didn't consider it on par with Fitzhugh's other work.

2. Edward Lucie-Smith, *The Art of Caricature* (Ithaca, N.Y.: Cornell University Press, 1981), 9–13; hereafter cited in the text as Lucie-Smith.

3. Wolfgang Kayser, *The Grotesque in Art and Literature,* trans. U. Weisstein (Bloomington: Indiana University Press, 1963), hereafter cited in the text as Kayser; and Werner Hoffman, *Caricature from Leonardo to Picasso* (London: John Calder, 1957), hereafter cited in the text as Hoffman.

4. Northrop Frye, *The Anatomy of Criticism* (Princeton, N.J.: Princeton University Press, 1957), 236–39.

5. James Merrill, letter to the author, 2 July 1988, in which he says, "I had been rather miffed by Louise and Sandra's takeoff on a poem of mine in 'Suzuki Beane,' but this was ancient history by then [ca. 1966–67]." He and Fitzhugh met at Bard in 1948, where he was a first-year instructor in English and her advisor.

6. Reviews of *Bang, Bang, You're Dead!*: *Bulletin of the Center for Children's Books* 22 (1 January 1969): 174; *Library Journal* 94 (15 June 1969): 2496; and *Teacher* 96 (January 1979): 65.

7. Review of *Bang, Bang, You're Dead!*, *Publishers Weekly*, 31 March 1969, 57.

8. Here again Fitzhugh's fiction becomes heavily autobiographical. Many of her friends commented on her never overcoming her loss of her mother and on her need for mothering, which, nevertheless, she found very difficult to accept. Fredericka Fulton Leser spoke of holding Louise nearly all of one weekend; Alixe Gordin, of how difficult it was for Louise to let anyone touch her and yet of how enormous Louise's need was for mothering.

Chapter Three

1. Reviews of *Harriet the Spy*: *Book Week*, 10 January 1965, 18; *Christian Science Monitor*, 25 February 1965, 7; and *Horn Book* 41 (February 1965), 74–76.

2. Review of *Harriet the Spy, Times Literary Supplement*, 5 July 1974, 715.

3. Francis Molson, "Another Look at *Harriet the Spy*," *Elementary English* 51 (October 1974): 967; hereafter cited in the text as Molson.

4. Hamida Bosmajian, "Louise Fitzhugh's *Harriet the Spy*: Nonsense and Sense," in *Touchstones: Reflections on the Best in Children's Literature*, ed. Perry Nodelman (West Lafayette, Ind.: Children's Literature Association Publications, 1985), 76; hereafter cited in the text as Bosmajian.

5. Lissa Paul, "The Feminist Writer as Heroine in *Harriet the Spy*," *Lion and the Unicorn* 13 (June 1989): 67–73; hereafter cited in the text as Paul.

6. Virginia Wolf, "*Harriet the Spy*: Milestone/Masterpiece?" *Children's Literature* 4 (1975): 120–26; hereafter cited in the text as Wolf.

7. M. E. Kerr, *Me Me Me Me Me* (New York: Harper & Row, 1983); hereafter cited in the text as Kerr.

8. Roni Natov and Geraldine DeLuca, "Discovering Contemporary Classics: An Interview with Ursula Nordstrom," *Lion and the Unicorn* 3 (Spring 1979): 124–25; hereafter cited in the text as Natov and DeLuca. Here Nordstrom describes her mentoring of Fitzhugh.

9. See the following for a discussion of the romantic view of the child: Peter Coveney, *Poor Monkey: The Child in Literature* (London: Rockliff, 1957), especially chap. 1, "The 'Cult of Sensibility' and the 'Romantic Child,'" 1–14; Hoxie Neale Fairchild, *The Noble Savage: A Study in Romantic Naturalism* (New York: Russell & Russell, 1961), especially chap. 10, "The Child of Nature and the Noble Savage," 365–85; and Robert Pattison, *The Child Figure in English Literature* (Athens: University of Georgia Press, 1978), especially chap. 3, "The Sentimental Aspects of the Child Figure: Wordsworth as Heretic," 47–75.

10. See Ihab Hassan's *Radical Innocence: Studies in the Contemporary Novel* (Princeton, N.J.: Princeton University Press, 1961) for a discussion of how the tradition of the innocent as God's spy continues to function in more recent novels.

11. This is the essential subject of Beebe's book—thus the title *Ivory Towers and Sacred Founts*. See also Meyer Abrams, *The Mirror and the Lamp: Romantic Theory and the Critical Tradition* (New York: Oxford University Press, 1953); Paul Cantor, *Creature and Creator: Mythmaking and English Romanticism* (Cambridge: Cambridge University Press, 1984); Milton C. Nahm, *The Artist as Creator: An Essay on Human Freedom* (Baltimore: Johns Hopkins University Press, 1956); and Dorothy L. Sayers, *The Mind of the Maker* (New York: Harcourt, Brace, 1941).

12. For example, Gilbert and Gubar, Hatterer, Hedges and Wendt, and Hiatt. Also Judy Chicago, *Through the Flower: My Struggle as a Woman Artist* (Garden City, N.Y.: Doubleday, 1977), and Carol Pearson and Katherine Pope, *The Female Hero in American and British Literature* (New York: R. R. Bowker, 1981).

13. See Alexander Thomas and Stella Chess, *Temperament and Development* (New York: Brunner/Mazel, 1977), 21–24 and 257–58. The propensity for introversion is measured in the child's instinctive withdrawal from, not approach to, new people, places, or things. See also A. H. Buss and R. Plomin, *A Temperament Theory of Personality Development* (New York: John Wiley & Sons, 1975), and Jerome Kagan and H. Moss, *Birth to Maturity* (New York: John Wiley & Sons, 1962).

14. See Rollo May's *Man's Search for Himself* (New York: W. W. Norton, 1953) and Erich Fromm's *The Art of Loving* (New York: Harper & Row, 1957) for discussion of self-love as the basis of love of others.

15. Two excellent studies that acknowledge both the positive and the negative results of shame are John Bradshaw, *Healing the Shame That Binds You,* (Deerfield Beach, Fla.: Health Communications, 1988), hereafter cited in the text as Bradshaw; and Carl D. Schneider, *Shame, Exposure, and Privacy* (Boston: Beacon Press, 1977).

16. See William Damon, *The Moral Child: Nurturing Children's Natural Moral Growth* (New York: Free Press, 1988), especially 10–17, but also chap. 2, "Empathy, Shame, and Guilt," 13–29.

17. This is the thesis of Anthony Storr's *Solitude*.

Chapter Four

1. Review of *The Long Secret, Library Journal* 90 (December 1965): 5513.

2. Reviews of *The Long Secret: New Yorker,* 4 December 1965, 218;

New Statesman, 21 May 1976, 687; *Book Week,* 31 October 1965, 20 and 41; and *New York Times Book Review,* 21 November 1965, 56 and 58.

3. Review of *The Long Secret, Saturday Review,* 11 December 1965, 45.

4. Isabel Quigly, review of *The Long Secret, Times Literary Supplement,* 19 September 1975, 1051.

5. Review of *The Long Secret, Best Sellers,* 1 December 1965, 356.

6. See Hedges and Wendt, *In Her Own Image: Women Working in the Arts;* Hiatt, *The Way Women Write;* and Jane Tompkins, *Sensational Designs: The Cultural Work of American Fiction 1790–1860* (New York: Oxford University Press, 1985).

Chapter Five

1. Review of *Nobody's Family Is Going to Change, Psychology Today,* 8 April 1975, 108.

2. Review of *Nobody's Family Is Going to Change, Publishers Weekly,* 4 November 1974, 68.

3. Reviews of *Nobody's Family Is Going to Change: Bulletin of the Center for Children's Books* 28 (May 1975): 146; *Booklist,* 1 February 1975, 570; *New York Times Book Review,* 1 December 1974, 9; and *Horn Book* 51 (April 1975): 146.

4. Reviews of *Nobody's Family Is Going to Change: Times Literary Supplement,* 2 April 1976, 375; *Language Arts* 52 (November 1975): 1169; *Booklist,* 15 March 1975, 766; *Childhood Education* 52 (October 1975): 32; *Journal of Reading* 19 (January 1976): 330.

5. Virginia L. Wolf, "A Novel of Children's Liberation," *Children's Literature* 5 (1976): 271.

6. Wayne Booth, *The Rhetoric of Fiction* (Chicago: University of Chicago Press, 1961), 42–50ff.

Chapter Six

1. Review of *Sport, New York Times Book Review,* 3 June 1979, 44; Nodelman, 141; and Gordin, personal correspondence, 11 August 1988.

2. Reviews of *Sport; Language Arts* 57 (January 1980): 85, and *Publishers Weekly,* 25 June 1979, 123.

3. Reviews of *Sport: Booklist,* 25 May 1979, 1438; *Best Sellers* 39 (November 1979): 289; *New Yorker,* 3 December 1979, 212; and *Childhood Education* 56 (January 1980): 169.

4. Northrop Frye, *The Secular Scripture: A Study in the Structure*

of Romance (Cambridge: Harvard University Press, 1976), especially the chapters "The Bottomless Dream: Themes of Descent" and *"Quis Hic Locus?*: Themes of Ascent."

Chapter Seven

1. The reviews already discussed point out the differences, as do comments by friends. *The Tap Dance Kid* has not yet been discussed. To say that it is a musical version of *Nobody's Family Is Going to Change* is perhaps to make my point about differences. It is also Willie's story, rather than Emma's, and much lighter in tone than the novel. This same difference in tone was striking in the production of *Harriet the Spy* by the Children's Theatre in Minneapolis. All of the dark underside of the novel was lost, principally because of the cutting necessary to stage it. As the reviewer in the *Minneapolis Star Tribune* put it, the play "captures so little of the texture, resonance and depth that make the book special," 8 February 1988, 8E.

2. One might also assume that something wonderful is yet to be published or produced. Lois Morehead says that there are other things; Charlotte Zolotow praised "The Owl and the Lark"; Mrs. Morehead and other friends would like to see films or other plays based on Fitzhugh's work, including "Mother Sweet, Father Sweet."

3. S. E. Hinton, *The Outsiders* (New York: Viking, 1967); Paul Zindel, *The Pigman* (New York: Harper & Row, 1968); Norma Klein, *Mom, the Wolf Man, and Me* (New York: Pantheon, 1972); Sandra Scoppetone, *Trying Hard to Hear You* (New York: Harper & Row, 1974); and Robert Cormier, *After the First Death* (New York: Pantheon, 1979).

4. Eleanor Estes, *The Moffats* (New York: Harcourt Brace, 1941); *The Middle Moffat* (New York: Harcourt Brace, 1942); and *Rufus M* (New York: Harcourt Brace, 1943).

5. Eleanor Estes, *Ginger Pye* (New York: Harcourt Brace, 1951).

6. Eleanor Estes, *The Alley* (New York: Harcourt, Brace & World, 1964); reviews of *The Alley, Book Week,* 1 November 1964, 16; *Commonweal* 81 (6 November 1964): 206; *New York Review of Books,* 3 December 1964, 14; *New York Times Review of Books,* part 2, 1 November 1964, 36; and *Saturday Review,* 7 November 1964, 53.

7. See Barbara Herrnstein Smith, "Contingencies of Value," in *Canons,* ed. Robert von Hallberg (Chicago: University of Chicago Press, 1983), 33–34 (hereafter cited in the text as Smith) and Tompkins, 200, which challenge the notion of a canon by exploring the ways in which a canonized book influences the culture and thereby perpetuates its status.

8. Judy Blume's *Are You There God, It's Me, Margaret* (Scarsdale, N.Y.: Bradbury, 1970) and *Deenie* (Scarsdale, N.Y.: Bradbury, 1973) are the best examples, although, certainly, some of her other novels are similar.

9. Althea Horner's *Being and Loving* (Northvale, N.J.: Jason Aronson, 1986).

Selected Bibliography

Primary Works

Books

Bang, Bang, You're Dead! (with Sandra Scoppetone). New York: Harper & Row, 1969.
Harriet the Spy. New York: Harper & Row, 1964.
I Am Three. Illustrated by Susanna Natti. New York: Delacorte, 1982.
I Am Five. New York: Delacorte, 1978.
I Am Four. Illustrated by Susan Bonner. New York: Delacorte, 1982.
The Long Secret. New York: Harper & Row, 1965.
Nobody's Family Is Going to Change. New York: Farrar, Straus & Giroux, 1974.
Sport. New York: Delacorte, 1979.
Suzuki Beane (with Sandra Scoppetone). New York: Doubleday, 1961.

Unpublished Materials

Amelia. Manuscript.
Crazybaby. Manuscript.
I Am Six. Manuscript.
Mother Sweet, Father Sweet. Manuscript.
The Owl and the Lark. Manuscript.

Secondary Works

Selected Reviews

Bang, Bang, You're Dead!

Bulletin of the Center for Children's Books 22 (1 January 1969): 174.
Library Journal 94 (15 June 1969): 2496.
Publishers Weekly, 31 March 1969, 57.
Teacher 96 (January 1979): 65.

Harriet the Spy

Book Week, 10 January 1965, 18.
Christian Science Monitor, 25 February 1965, 7.
Times Literary Supplement, 5 July 1974, 715.
Viguers, Ruth Hill. *Horn Book* 41 (February 1965): 74–76.

The Long Secret

Best Sellers, 1 December 1965, 356.
Book Week, 31 October 1965, 20 and 41.
Library Journal 90 (December 1965): 5513.
New Statesman, 21 May 1976, 687.
New Yorker, 4 December 1965, 218.
New York Times Book Review, 21 November 1965, 56 and 58.
Saturday Review, 11 December 1965, 45.
Times Literary Supplement, 19 September 1975, 1051.

Nobody's Family Is Going to Change

Booklist, 1 February 1975, 570; 15 March 1975, 766.
Bulletin of the Center for Children's Books 28 (May 1975): 146.
Childhood Education 52 (October 1975): 32.
Horn Book 51 (April 1975): 146.
Journal of Reading 19 (January 1976): 330.
Language Arts 52 (November 1975): 1169.
New York Times Book Review, 1 December 1974, 9.
Psychology Today, 8 April 1975, 108.
Publishers Weekly, 4 November 1974, 68.
Times Literary Supplement, 2 April 1976, 375.

Sport

Best Sellers 39 (November 1979): 289.
Booklist, 25 May 1979, 1438.
Childhood Education 56 (January 1980): 169.
Language Arts 57 (January 1980): 85.
New Yorker, 3 December 1979, 212.
New York Times Book Review, 3 June 1979, 44.
Publishers Weekly, 25 June 1979, 123.

Criticism

"A Tribute to Louise Fitzhugh, 1928–74." St. James Church, New York.
Photocopy. Rev. Willoughby Newton presided and tributes were

given by Maurice Sendak, Peter Taylor, James Merrill, Fredericka
Fulton Leser, Francis Hines, Julien Levy, Marijane Meeker, Evelyn
Roberts Patterson, and Elizabeth Baker Crabtree. Quotations from
Fitzhugh's work were read by Sloane Shelton.

Bosmajian, Hamida. "Louise Fitzhugh's *Harriet the Spy*: Nonsense and
Sense." In vol. 1 of *Touchstones: Reflections on the Best in Children's
Literature,* edited by Perry Nodelman, 71–82. West Lafayette, Ind.
Children's Literature Association Publications, 1985; analyzes the
metaphysical, social, and psychological implications of the novel, focusing on the absence of connections (the nonsense) in Harriet's
world.

Finke, Kate. "Breakdown of the Family: Fictional Case Studies in Contemporary Novels for Young People." *The Lion and the Unicorn* 3
(Winter 1979–80): 86–95; explores the inability of families to sus-
tain themselves and to nurture children in Isabelle Holland's *The
Man without a Face* (1972), Susan Terris's *The Drowning Boy*
(1972), Fitzhugh's *Nobody's Family Is Going to Change* (1974), and
Vera and Bill Cleaver's *Where the Lilies Bloom* (1969).

Kerr, M. E. *Me Me Me Me Me.* New York: Harper & Row, 1983; autobiography of those parts of Marijane Meaker's life that influenced her
career as a children's writer; relevant here for its exploration of her
friendship with Fitzhugh as a possible source of Fitzhugh's inspiration for Harriet.

Molson, Francis. "Another Look at *Harriet the Spy*." *Elementary English*
51 (October 1974): 963–70; examines the novel in terms of its portrait of the genesis of a writer.

————"Portrait of the Young Writer in Children's Fiction." *The Lion and
the Unicorn* 1 (Fall 1977): 77–99; explores the connections between
each protagonist's development as a person and as a writer in Fitzhugh's *Harriet the Spy,* Irene Hunt's *Up a Road Slowly,* Jean Little's
Look through My Window, Eleanor Cameron's *A Room Full of Win-
dows,* and Mollie Hunter's *A Sound of Chariots.*

Natov, Roni, and Geraldine DeLuca. "Discovering Contemporary Classics: An Interview with Ursula Nordstrom." *Lion and the Unicorn* 3
(Spring 1979), 119–35; highlights of Nordstrom's career working as
editor at Harper Junior Books with Fitzhugh, Sendak, and Kerr,
among others.

Nodelman, Perry. "Louise Fitzhugh." In *American Writers for Children
Since 1960,* edited by Glenn E. Estes, 133–42. Vol. 52, *Dictionary of
Literary Biography.* Detroit: Gale, 1986; groundbreaking analysis of
all of Fitzhugh's published work as satire, with a brief overview of
Fitzhugh's life.

Paul, Lissa. "The Feminist Writer as Heroine in *Harriet the Spy*." *Lion
and the Unicorn* 13 (June 1989): 67–73; argues that Fitzhugh was

ahead of her time in her portrait of Harriet as a writer who is not only free of many of the female stereotypes, but is also subversive of patriarchy in her spying and gossip.

Wolf, Virgina L. *"Harriet the Spy*: Milestone/Masterpiece?" *Children's Literature* 4 (1975): 120–26; argues that the novel's psychological realism and thematic resonance make it both a milestone and a masterpiece.

————. "A Novel of Children's Liberation." *Children's Literature* 5 (1976): 207–72; examines the many social problems that oppress children in *Nobody's Family Is Going to Change* and argues that the excessive attention to these problems weakens the novel.

————. "Readers of Alice: My Children, Meg Murry, and Harriet M. Welsch." *Children's Literature Association Quarterly* 13 (Fall 1988): 135–37; attempts to describe the implied reader of Lewis Carroll's Alice books by exploring the commonalities among real and fictional children who are fond of the books and by contrasting them with children who don't like the books.

Index

The Author

Virginia L. Wolf is professor of English and special assistant to the chancellor at the University of Wisconsin–Stout. She received her B.S. in English Education and her M.A. and Ph.D. in English from the University of Kansas and has taught at all levels of education for nearly 30 years, specializing for more than 20 years in the teaching of literature for young people. Her essays have appeared in such publications as *Children's Literature, Children's Literature Association Quarterly, Children's Literature in Education, Studies in the Literary Imagination,* and *The Dictionary of Literary Biography.* She is on the editorial board for *Children's Literature Association Quarterly* and *Children's Literature in Education.*

The Editor

Ruth K. MacDonald is a professor of English and head of the Department of English and Philosophy at Purdue University. She received her B.A. and M.A. in English from the University of Connecticut, her Ph.D. in English from Rutgers University, and her M.B.A. from the University of Texas at El Paso. To Twayne's United States and English Authors series she has contributed the volumes on Louisa May Alcott, Beatrix Potter, and Dr. Seuss. She is the author of *Literature for Children in England and America. 1646–1774* (1982).